Smokin' Southern BBQ

Smokin'★ SOUTHERN BBQ

Barbecue Recipes and Techniques from *Around the South*

Glenn Connaughton

Photography by Iain Bagwell

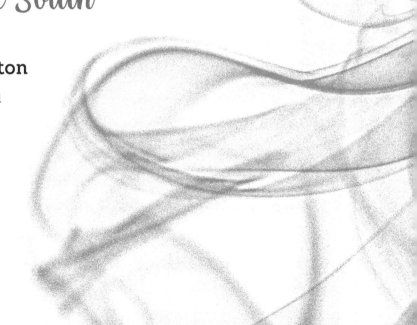

ROCKRIDGE PRESS

Interior and Cover Designer: Darren Samuel
Art Producer: Sue Bischofberger
Editor: Justin Hartung
Production Editor: Matt Burnett
Production Manager: Holly Haydash

Photography © 2021 Iain Bagwell; food styling by Loren Wood
Author photograph courtesy of Vida Connaughton
Cover: Loaf Pan Chicken, page 164; KC Brisket, page 54
Hardcover ISBN 978-1-63878-499-9 | Paperback ISBN: 978-1-64739-832-3 | eBook ISBN: 978-1-64739-529-2
R0

To my wife, Vida, who is my best friend and partner for life, and to my children, whom I hope I have taught the true meaning of barbecue.

CONTENTS

INTRODUCTION

I have been interested in cooking for as long as I can remember. Growing up in New York City with my mother, I was always curious about what she was cooking, and I wanted to pitch in. Eventually, this led to me cooking my own dishes and experimenting with flavors. During summer barbecues with my dad, I was fascinated by how fire could be used to cook such tasty meat. Later, I was exposed to many new cooking methods through cooking shows. I was mesmerized by Bobby Flay and his *Grillin' & Chillin'* series. That's when I knew I was hooked. I figured that if this other guy from New York City could barbecue, then so could I. Over the next 10 years, with my wife, Vida, by my side, I attempted to perfect my craft, focusing on Kansas City and Texas styles. When we finally attended our first barbecue competition in 2009, conversations with many of the contestants provided a wealth of knowledge. I could not believe how openly the pitmasters shared their experiences, brought me behind the scenes, and showed me the magic that happened behind the curtain. Shortly after, we started our competition and barbecue seasoning brand, Revolution Barbecue, with the idea that no one type of barbecue was the right style. We tried to incorporate as many different styles into our dishes as possible—how revolutionary!

Growing up a Yankee in New Jersey and New York, I never really understood what the true spirit of a Southern barbecue was: a community gathered around the enjoyment of low and slow cooked meats. The bond between our family and friends is centered around this tradition, and it's brought all of us closer together. I truly hope that this book provides a straightforward introduction to each regional style of Southern barbecue. I'll share authentic recipes for proteins and rubs, plus tips and tricks to help you achieve greater barbecue mastery as you, your friends, and your family take a journey similar to mine.

One

Cooking with Smoke

Very few words act as a verb, a noun, and an adjective, but "barbecue" can. This versatility is one of barbecue's most attractive features. Learning to barbecue is a slow and time-consuming process, but the lessons along the way are both rewarding and delicious. People from all over the world have their own low and slow cooking techniques, and many claim to be the first to use their preferred methods, but this book will celebrate what we know today as Southern barbecue.

True Barbecue

While barbecue may seem emblematic of the cuisine of the United States, food historians generally agree it originated in the Caribbean, where the Taino people cooked barbacoa over coals on a grill made of wood. The style of cooking was brought from the islands to the continent by Spanish conquistadors, and within a few hundred years, the technique was well established in what became the Southern United States.

During the 18th century, plantation owners regularly held large barbecues called "pig pickin's." Because pigs were cheaper and required less maintenance than other livestock, pork became the primary meat at these barbecues.

Barbecue became the mainstay for large gatherings like church festivals, neighborhood parties, and even political rallies. In 1829, President Andrew Jackson of Tennessee had the first official barbecue at the White House, spawning a new era of political campaigning at barbecues. It is even said that William Henry Harrison, the ninth president of the United States, used barbecues during his campaign to show that he was a "man of the people," helping him win the 1840 election.

After the Civil War, the millions of African Americans who moved away from the South during the Great Migration spread their barbecue traditions throughout the country. Around the turn of the 20th century, the pit men that ran these barbecue events started opening their own stands on the weekend after working a full week on the farm. The typical barbecue joint was just a shack consisting of corrugated tin walls and a roof over a concrete slab floor. Eventually, tables and chairs were added, leading to a full-time business. With the advent of the automobile, barbecue joints became roadside stands that offered cheap, filling, and delicious meals. The traveling clientele also helped spread the word about the great food, driving more business and, eventually, the conversion into a full-fledged restaurant.

Modern barbecue saw explosive growth after the end of World War II with a national movement promoting suburban home ownership and a barbecue in every backyard. The barbecue grill and smoker business nearly quadrupled in the four years after 1951. This drive to cook outdoors was deemed a purely American quality and helped create a revolution of sorts in the industry. With the South's extensive experience in barbecue, people started to flock to barbecue restaurants in the region, aspiring to one day cook in their backyards like these pitmasters did at their 'cue joints.

Today, barbecue varies by region, with many differences in style primarily influenced by the various preferences of European immigrants to the United States. There are arguably eight major styles of Southern barbecue in the United States, with many more variations beyond the scope of this book. The eight we'll be covering are: Texas Hill Country, Kansas City, St. Louis, Memphis, Kentucky, North Carolina, South Carolina, and Alabama.

Classic Woods

When it comes to smoking meats, the right type of wood is one of the most critical ingredients. Unless you're using a pellet smoker, I recommend starting your fire with charcoal, and then using wood chunks to create the smoke. I suggest using wood chunks instead of chips for long cooks; they will last longer. The chips are typically great for short, quick bursts of smoke and not meant for longer low and slow recipes.

When selecting charcoal, only use lump hardwood charcoal or charcoal briquettes with no added flavoring or lighter fluid. The charcoal is just a heat source;

the wood should provide the smoke flavor. For barbecue, you'll want to use hardwood, which comes from deciduous trees (such as nut and fruit trees) that shed their leaves each year. Softwoods come from coniferous trees and never shed their leaves—think pine, spruce, and fir. Softwood trees have a high resin level, giving off a pungent and bitter smell that will permeate your meats. Hardwoods produce carbonyl compounds when they smoke, adding to the caramelized flavor of smoked meats.

There are dozens of woods out on the market, but I will focus on those typically used in Southern barbecue. I encourage you to create your own secret blend of wood that sets your barbecue apart from others. For pork and beef, I find that an equal mix of mesquite, hickory, and cherry (known as MHC in the biz) is a great go-to blend. For chicken, I suggest lighter fruit woods, such as apple, while turkey could use a bit more smoke through a combination of hickory and applewood. If you are looking for that Texas barbecue flavor, I suggest a blend of oak and mesquite.

With the explosion of barbecue in recent years, you can find barbecue supply sections in just about every supermarket. When it comes to wood chunks, try to avoid mass-produced woods because the age of the wood is unknown and the product can be extremely dried out. I also recommend looking for local firewood shops that specialize in barbecue wood chunks. These establishments typically cut their own wood, which is sourced locally.

Here is a breakdown of some of the most popular woods for smoking:

Alder: This wood is not native to the Southern United States, but I mention it here because it is excellent for smoking fish. It adds a light note of smoke without overpowering the fish.

Apple: Providing a mild and sweet smoke to the meat, applewood pairs well with chicken, pork, and turkey. Given its mild nature, it can take a while for applewood to deliver a deep flavor, so it is best used for recipes with long cook times.

Cherry: With a mild and fruity flavor, this wood provides a beautiful smoke ring when used for long cook times. It is one of my favorite woods to use on pork shoulder, ribs, or ham (especially with a brown sugar glaze).

Hickory: Used extensively on large cuts of brisket and pork and conveying a savory, smoky flavor, this wood is a staple in Southern barbecue. Overusing hickory can add a bitter flavor in your meat, so only use it for the first four to five hours of smoking.

Mesquite: Known as the most intensely flavored hardwood, mesquite can create a strong, almost ashtray-like flavor if overused. I suggest using it sparingly, one wood chunk at a time. It is best used in a blend, such as MHC. This combo pairs well with most large red meat cuts, such as brisket, clod, or roast.

Oak: Producing a medium-intensity smoke, oak is always great to have around. It pairs well with most meats, and I highly suggest it for beginners. It tends to burn hot and needs to be replenished often, or you can mix it with other slower burning woods, such as cherry or maple.

Pecan: This wood provides a rich, nutty, and sweet flavor that's less intense than hickory. Still, you'll want to use it sparingly for long cook times to avoid creating an undesirable bitter taste. It pairs nicely with most poultry and pork ribs.

Pits Primer

Barbecue pits get their name from the indigenous Taino method of cooking over trenches dug into the ground. These pits were filled with hot coals, then covered with a grate made of sticks and branches, which elevated the meat above the coals. Modern pit and smoker designs vary widely but are all designed to do the same thing: smoke meat. The type of smoker you choose will depend on your budget, skill level, and how much time you want to dedicate to tending the fire.

When selecting a smoker, your budget should be the first thing to consider. I do not recommend dropping a few thousand dollars on a new smoker, especially if you are just getting started. Beginner barbecuers will be served just fine by less expensive home pits.

Next, think about what meats you will be cooking and how many people you would typically cook for. Will you be hosting a kegger every weekend to watch the big game, or will you just be cooking for your family? This will help determine what size smoker you will need. The quality of the materials is also critical. Is the cooker a single wall or a double wall? Is the metal thin and flexible, or hard and rigid? The thickness of the metal—look for a double-walled construction—is usually a good indicator of the quality of the unit and will be critical to the efficiency of the smoker. Lastly, I would recommend looking at the airflow of the unit. Do the size and location of the vents seem to allow for easy airflow? Will they allow the smoke to traverse from the firebox, over the meat, and then out the chimney?

If you have a barbecue provisions store near you that fires up the grill each weekend for public demonstrations, I suggest seeking them out. Just like test driving a car, a live demo of a new smoker can be invaluable. Go back to the store a few times and see if they use the same unit for each demo to provide food samples to the public. If they use the same smoker every weekend, that's a good indication of a quality unit and gives you insights into what a professional would use.

Now that you have a basic understanding of what you are looking for in a smoker, let's dive into the six main categories of smokers.

Kettle Grill

The kettle-style grill is arguably the most iconic American grill and is typically credited with the boom of the backyard barbecue that started in the 1950s. The story goes that George Stephen invented the kettle grill in 1952 while working at Chicago's Weber Brothers Metal Works. They specialized in making buoys, and George, being a passionate griller, cut one in half, added three legs, and put a handle on top, resulting in the easily recognizable backyard mainstay. This multi-tasking grill can be used as an offset smoker by placing coals and wood chunks on one side of the grill and your meat on the other. Most grills in this category tend to be smaller, limiting the amount of food you can cook at once.

Gas Grill

Not typically synonymous with the low and slow smoking method, a gas grill is usually used to grill meats hot and fast. If you have a gas grill with multiple zones, you could fashion one as an offset smoker by turning the burners on one side to low and placing wood chips over the flame in an aluminum foil packet with perforated holes. Then, place your meat on the other side of the grill (the burners under the meat should be off).

Pellet Smoker

Pellet smokers made a huge splash in the 2000s, but they've actually been around since about 1985, when Joe Traeger first introduced the Traeger pellet grill. These units take a set-it-and-forget-it approach to cooking with wood. A true pellet grill is heated solely by wood pellets, with no coals or gas, and is lit using a heated rod that ignites the wood pellets. Many units today offer smartphone apps that can manage the grill, set timers, create alerts, and even load preprogrammed schedules to your smoker.

Bullet Smoker

The bullet-style smoker is generally a great entry-level smoker, though I have seen many an experienced barbecue team, including our own, cook with a bullet. The design is similar to the kettle grill with a long cylinder in the middle, increasing the height of the unit. The firebox sits below the meat, but the drip pan acts as a deflector shield to protect the meat from the heat. The drip pan can also be filled with water or other liquids to keep the meat moist and infuse it with flavor. The firebox can typically be accessed through a side door, making it easy to check the coals or refill it without lifting the lid. There are dampers on the top and bottom of the unit to control the airflow and temperature.

Kamado Smoker

The kamado smoker is one of the oldest appliances for cooking and smoking meats. Ceramic and clay pot cooking was invented 3,000 years ago in China and exported to Japan, where the smoker was dubbed *kamado* (meaning "stove"). The modern-day version is a ceramic-lined, kettle-shaped cooker capable of generating large amounts of heat with little fuel. The kamado smoker is versatile; one could smoke at low temperatures as well as above 600 degrees Fahrenheit in certain models. As the heat emanates from below the meat, a diffuser plate protects the meat from direct heat. Most of the units require the meat and diffuser plate be removed to refill charcoal and wood chunks, although kamado smokers are quite efficient and can typically go for 8 to 10 hours without needing additional fuel.

Offset Smoker

To many old-school purists, the offset smoker, also known as a "stick burner," is the only way to smoke barbecue. The origin of the offset barrel smoker is rumored to lie with oil workers who converted old 55-gallon drums into cookers, with a firebox built in one chamber and a space for the meat in another. Most offset smokers are horizontal, although they can be found in vertical configurations as well. Both situate the firebox below the main barrel, hence the name, "offset." Depending on the size of the firebox, either wood or charcoal is placed in the firebox and lit. The heat and smoke flows through a vent between the two chambers, circulating the smoke around the meat before exiting a chimney on the opposite side of the unit. The heat is controlled by vents on the firebox and at the top of the chimney. Depending on the size of your offset smoker, some manufacturers use what is called "reverse flow," where the chimney is on the firebox end of the unit. Reverse flow causes the smoke to travel to the far end of the smoker, and then reverse direction to flow back to the chimney. Baffles or convection plates direct the airflow. An offset smoker requires more hands-on interaction to maintain a consistent temperature. However, sitting around maintaining the fire while swapping barbecue stories with a friend is, arguably, what barbecue is all about.

What about Electric Smokers?

Generally, I do not recommend an electric smoker to cook barbecue. The electric smoker generates heat with an electric coil, much like a home oven, with a small tray to place the wood chips for the smoky flavor. The wood chip tray is typically quite small and needs to be refilled every 30 to 60 minutes to provide any smoke flavor. The constant opening of the cooker to replenish the wood chips releases all the heat each time, creating a constant cycle of heating and cooling, which is not conducive to efficient cooking.

In My Toolbox

After you have selected your pit and decided on what smoking woods to use, it's time to gather your essential tools.

Notebook: You might be surprised to read that my number one smoking tool is my notebook. It is always by my side and contains notes on nearly every cook (pitmaster lingo for a cooking project). It's so integral to my cooking that I call it "the bible." Have you ever added a pinch of this and a dash of that while cooking, only to end up with one of the best things you ever made? Or tasted a glorious dish that you have no idea how to recreate? This is why I keep a journal—so I don't have to rely on memory for the details.

Digital Thermometer: Forget what you might have heard about the jiggle technique to see if your brisket is done; you will never really know if you do not check the temperature. I've found that the top reason why people are dissatisfied with the results of their cook is because they cooked the meat for 10 hours—"because the recipe said to"—but never actually checked the meat's internal temperature.

When it comes to meat, recipes can't account for the variations found in any one piece of meat, which is why a thermometer won't steer you wrong.

Heat-Resistant Rubber Gloves: I recommend a good pair of gloves made from food-grade neoprene rubber. Opt for longer ones that reach your forearms, which will assist with carrying large pieces of meats, such as brisket. Even though some may think it's cool to go back to work and show off the burns they received while mastering their backyard cook, it sure feels a lot better to avoid getting burned in the first place.

Disposable Aluminum Pans: These are indispensable when used as water pans to regulate temperate, and they are also a great way to serve your food at your barbecue event. If you're wrapping your meats during the cook, place the meat in the pan and cover it tightly with foil to collect all the juices. They are very resistant and can survive multiple uses, saving you money.

Spring-Loaded Tongs: I like a pair of small metal tongs for pulling and a larger pair to lift whole pieces of meat. Fairly new to the scene are barbecue turners: large, heavy-duty spatulas that are helpful for transitioning hot meat to an aluminum pan. Using tongs in this case may tear the meat rather than lifting it.

Compression Sprayer: These pump-top sprayers are worth their weight in gold when it comes to keeping your meat moist during the cooking process. Add liquid to the bottle, tighten the lid, and pump the top handle until pressure builds up. Then, just pull the trigger, and a steady mist of liquid will spray out without causing wrist cramps. Think of an old-school garden sprayer but made for your barbecue.

Two

Southern Know-How

One of the most appealing things about smoking meat? The process itself is quite simple. That said, you'll need to learn a few tips and tricks to master true Southern barbecue. I'll walk you through some of the most popular cuts of meats to smoke and provide must-know info for working with each of them. You'll also learn how to take the flavor of your barbecue to new heights with brines, marinades, rubs, and sauces.

Barbecue Wisdom

Here are a few tried-and-true tips to make your barbecue as easy (and tasty) as possible.

1. Make sure that all of your spices are out, the smoker is clean, your fire source is staged, and all of your tools are ready to go.

2. Keep your meat refrigerated until it is time to prep; cold meat absorbs more smoke.

3. Kick up the flavor with either a brine, injection, rub, or a combination of these. Be careful not to over-season. The true measure of good barbecue is the flavor and moistness of the meat.

4. Light the fire according to your cooker's instructions. For most cookers, this will require lighting charcoal topped with wood chunks. Be sure not to introduce any chemicals (such as lighter fluid) that can find their way into the flavor of the meat.

5. Get smoking. Be sure to keep an eye on your fire. You want to ensure that the fire does not go out and that you don't add too many wood chunks. The ultimate fire should produce a clear to blue-white smoke. Never add unlit charcoal to your fire; doing so will cause soot to get into your food.

6. Always use a thermometer to test for doneness. Remember that every animal is unique and so is each piece of meat. Above all, you want your delicious smoked meat to be safe.

Pork

Pork is the cornerstone of Southern barbecue and has been essential to the region's economy for hundreds of years. The conquistadors brought pigs with them when they landed in places like Savannah, Georgia, and Tampa Bay, Florida, over 400 years ago, and pork eventually became a mainstay of the Southern diet.

Cuts

Pork shoulder is sometimes called pork butt or Boston butt (in colonial times, less expensive cuts of pork were shipped in barrels called butts).

Right below the pork shoulder is the picnic ham. Be on the lookout for a good, fat cap—a thin layer of fat just below the skin that will add moistness.

Moving down the animal, the next cut is the pork belly, where American bacon comes from. This cut can be found with or without the skin. Either way, look for a good ratio of fat to meat.

Baby back ribs are smaller than the spareribs found down near the belly. I prefer spareribs trimmed St. Louis style, where the tips are removed. Doing so not only provides a meatier bite but also allows more fat per bite, which translates into more flavor.

Finally, there is the ham, which is found on the rear leg of the animal. A whole ham includes both the butt (upper) and shank (lower) cuts of the leg. The shank has fewer pockets of fat to render down, meaning it's easier to carve and has a sweeter taste.

When shopping for pork, look for marbling and color. The more marbling the meat has, the more flavor it will offer. However, be on the lookout for large white chunks of fat, as those will not render when cooking. When it comes to color, "the redder, the better."

Never oversmoke pork, which has a very mild flavor. Ease into adding more wood chunks to your fire and look for a white- to blue-colored smoke.

Avoid harshly flavored woods like mesquite. Hickory, cherry, or applewood complement pork's mild flavor.

Trim most—but not all!—of the exterior fat from the meat. The flavorful bark on barbecue ribs is created when the rub adheres to the meat and not to the fat, but leaving on some fat will contribute to the flavor.

Beef

A smoky, juicy brisket is a Southern barbecue classic made famous by the pit-masters of Central Texas. However, don't overlook some of the other beef cuts available, like rib and shoulder cuts. The most commonly used beef grade in barbecue is USDA Choice, which has a decent amount of marbling that keeps the meat tender and juicy; it's also kind to your wallet.

Cuts

Brisket is synonymous with Texas barbecue. This cut is the chest muscle of the animal and is typically bought whole as a "packer brisket," meaning it includes both the point and the flat. When cooked low and slow, the flat is excellent for slicing, while the point makes for great chopped brisket or can even be cubed and served up as burnt ends.

Plate ribs are affectionately called "dinosaur ribs," given their huge size. Much prized for their marbling, plate ribs can be hard to find; check with your local butcher or shop online. Farther up the animal, you'll find the smaller chuck ribs.

Beef chuck comes from the cow's forequarter. This primal cut produces the seven-bone roast, the flat iron steak, and ground chuck, which makes for excellent burgers and chopped beef sandwiches.

Hot Tips

Keep the beef's surface moist but not wet for the best smoked flavor. I suggest using a compression sprayer with either apple juice or a fifty-fifty mix of apple cider vinegar and water. You can also mix a cola made from cane sugar (rather than high fructose corn syrup) with a little water.

Avoid over-trimming. You'll want to remove the surface fat, especially any hard fat, as it will not render down, and always remove any silver skin. To trim brisket, leave between ¼ and ½ inch of the fat cap; this will help provide moisture and allow a crust to form.

When cooking brisket, the fat side should face the heat source. If you're using a bullet, kamado, or pellet smoker, place the brisket fat-side down. If you're using any other type of smoker, cook the meat fat-side up.

Poultry

Much as how pigs made their way to the New World, the modern chicken owes its migration to the American South to European explorers and colonizers who brought them over during their expeditions. There are a few things to be aware of when considering poultry labels. The "hormone free" label is essentially redundant, as hormone-injected chicken has been illegal to sell in the United States since the 1950s. "Cage free" is only used to label chickens that are farmed to produce eggs. "Natural" means a food contains no artificial ingredients or added color and is only minimally processed, which can pretty much apply to all chicken. You should, however, avoid any chicken labeled "basted" or "self-basted." If you brine an already basted chicken, it will be extremely salty.

Cuts

My recommendation is to always purchase a whole bird and butcher it yourself, which only takes a little practice to master. A whole bird is less processed than chicken bought in parts; also, it's typically cheaper, and by butchering it yourself, you'll get more evenly sized pieces without the bone shards created by industrial saws.

Hot Tips

The most even way to cook a whole bird is to spatchcock it, also known as butterflying. To do so, place the bird breast-side down with the legs facing you. Remove the backbone by cutting along the sides of it with sharp poultry shears. Then, make an inch-long cut on each side of the interior breastbone, which will help with the flattening process. Turn the bird over, pull both breasts up with your fingers while pushing down with your thumbs, and then use the ball of your hand to flatten the entire bird.

Lamb

After the Tariff of 1816, when wool production exploded, sheep were abundant in the United States. Lamb was also a popular meat in Northern Mexico, which influenced much of Texas cuisine. After the Civil War, beef became readily available, and lamb declined in popularity. However, it can still be found in Central Texas barbecue joints, typically served as cabrito, and is enjoyed in Kentucky as smoked mutton with a Worcestershire dip.

Cuts

The most common cut of lamb found in the United States is the loin, which extends from the last rib to the hip area. This tender cut can be smoked—but typically for less than an hour.

The meat from the shoulder contains a fair amount of connective tissue, meaning it's ideal for low and slow cooking. It should be smoked to around 200 degrees Fahrenheit, and it's traditionally carved off the bone and chopped.

Leg of lamb is sold whole or broken into smaller roasts, which are typically deboned. I suggest using the whole leg when smoking low and slow to ensure that the connective tissue has not been trimmed away. The leg will need to be removed from the smoker at around 140 degrees Fahrenheit, which typically takes around three hours of smoking.

Hot Tips

Imported lamb is usually pasture fed on grasses, whereas domestic lamb typically feeds on grain for the last stage of its life. The grain finish will mute the lamb's flavor, leading to a sweeter taste. I am a huge supporter of shopping local, but, in my opinion, imported lamb just tastes better.

Lamb lends itself to a wide array of spices. Experiment with the flavors of Northern Mexico, such as ancho and guajillo chilies, the mustards and Worcestershire used in parts of Kentucky, or just go simple with salt and pepper.

Lamb can stand up to stronger-tasting wood smoke. Southern pitmasters traditionally smoke lamb with hickory, but the meat also pairs well with applewood for a sweeter taste or mesquite for a bolder, smokier finish. Feel free to experiment; just don't oversmoke lamb, which can make it tough and flavorless.

Robust Flavors

Brines, rubs, marinades, and sauces are all great for adding moisture and flavor to your meats. It is always smart to buy high quality and fresh ingredients when making your sauces and rubs.

Types

Marinades are best used to add flavor to the surface of smaller cuts of meat. They usually include some sort of acid, like vinegar or citrus juice, which helps tenderize the meat.

Brines add moisture and flavor to proteins that would typically dry out in the smoker. These are best used on poultry, pork, and certain lamb cuts that have limited amounts of fat.

Spice rubs are best for seasoning the outside of larger cuts of meat and can amp up the flavor of milder meats like chicken and pork. Typical spices in rubs include salt, pepper, and sugar.

Sauces are one of the most debated aspects of barbecue. Do you sauce or not sauce? Some purists feel that if you cooked the meat properly, no sauce is necessary, while others feel that it can enhance the flavors of the meats. This book includes plenty of sauce options.

Hot Tips

For brines, sauces, and spice rubs, use cane sugar, like turbinado or muscovado, rather than white sugar, which will likely burn and become bitter when smoked.

There are so many variations of paprika, including sweet, smoked, savory, and spicy. The bulk of paprika comes from Hungary, but give Spanish or Mexican paprika a try, too.

As soon as black pepper is ground, it begins to oxidize and lose flavor. When you grind it yourself, you ensure that it's fresh and can control the size of the grinds.

Don't be afraid to get creative by switching up various regions' marinades, rubs, and sauces. Remember, it's not always about the destination, but the journey.

Three

Texas Hill Country

The Story

Modern day Texas barbecue owes its roots mostly to Czech and German immigrants, who settled throughout Central Texas. Smoking meat was a way to preserve it from spoiling and extend its shelf life. Local wood like hickory, pecan, and mesquite was used. In the early 1800s, goat and lamb were the staple for barbecued meats, but beef became widely available after the Civil War. Prior to the 1900s, meat processors would give away briskets to barbecue joints when they purchased other cuts of meat. During that same time period, a large Jewish population moved to Texas; that community was already used to eating brisket, which only added to its popularity. Finally, Northern Mexico had a profound influence in the Texas 'cue scene with barbacoa and many other dishes.

Best-Kept Secrets

» There has been a recent resurgence in using butcher paper to wrap beef brisket later during the cook, and it's a great substitute for foil. This method is jokingly called "the Texas crutch." If you're using butcher paper, be sure that it's 100 percent food-grade butcher paper and contains no silicone or wax, which will come off at high temperatures and ruin your meat.

» Salt is one of the main ingredients in Texas Hill Country barbecue, so it's important to use the right kind. As most recipes measure salt by volume, it is important to use the same type of salt for each recipe and get to know its salinity so that you can adjust it to your taste. Be sure to use a coarse-grain kosher salt and not table salt, which can contain iodine and anticaking agents to assist its use in saltshakers but that don't help out at all while barbecuing.

Classic Sides

German potato salad is traditional in Central Texas. Served warm, this "salad" includes bacon and has a sweet-and-sour flavor due to the addition of brown sugar and apple cider vinegar.

Another dish indebted to German and Czech immigrants is mustard potato salad. Yellow mustard gives it a bright color and tangy flavor; Dijon-style mustard conveys a spicier flavor; and a German coarse-grain mustard provides a darker color and heartier flavor.

Originating from Tejano and Mexican cowboys, borracho beans sit in your smoker while you're cooking your meats. This process imparts an incredible smoky flavor and will help you one-up your neighbor at your next block party. Adding bacon, leftover brisket chunks, or pork rib meat will take this dish to a whole new level.

DALMATIAN RUB

MAKES 4½ CUPS

PREP TIME: 5 MINUTES

In the Republic of Texas, beef purists use what is affectionately called the Dalmatian Rub for most of their beef dishes. This simple rub is made of just salt and pepper—hence the name—but I like to add spices. If you make a larger batch, store it in a cool, dry place. The fresh-ground pepper will lose its potency over time, so make no more than you can use in a three-month period.

1 cup kosher salt

1 cup freshly ground black pepper

1 tablespoon granulated garlic (optional)

1 tablespoon granulated onion (optional)

1 tablespoon smoked paprika (optional)

1 tablespoon ground coriander (optional)

Mix all of the ingredients in a small, sealable plastic container.

Storage Tip: This rub can be stored in an airtight container for up to three months.

Experiment: Use any combination of the optional ingredients to put your own spin on this rub. I suggest only using the coriander on beef dishes, but all the other flavor combinations can be used on beef, pork, and lamb.

TEXAS RED SAUCE

MAKES 4½ CUPS
PREP TIME: 10 MINUTES
COOK TIME: 15 MINUTES

Traditional Texas Red Sauce is a well-seasoned mix of tomato ketchup, onions, peppers, and vinegar. It is thinner and less sweet than the Kansas City-style sauces found in modern grocery stores. The key to success with this sauce is to add the meat drippings to complement your plate of Texas beef.

2 tablespoons unsalted butter

1 cup finely chopped white onion

½ cup finely chopped green pepper

1½ cups apple cider vinegar

1 cup ketchup

1 cup water

½ cup white vinegar

¼ cup Worcestershire sauce

1 tablespoon red pepper flakes

1½ teaspoons ground cumin

1 teaspoon freshly ground black pepper

1 teaspoon chili powder

1 teaspoon kosher salt

½ teaspoon granulated garlic

½ teaspoon granulated onion

1. Heat the butter in a small saucepan over medium heat.

2. Add the onion and green pepper to the pan and cook until the onion is translucent.

3. Add all of the remaining ingredients to the pan and whisk until incorporated. Raise the temperature to medium-high heat and continue to slowly whisk. Once the sauce has begun to boil, remove it from the heat.

4. Allow the sauce to cool, then blend it in a food processor or blender until smooth.

Pro Advice: To take this sauce to the next level, take the drippings from your brisket or chopped beef and add it to the sauce. Return the sauce to low heat and allow it to simmer for 15 minutes. Serve warm.

MARKET-STYLE SMOKED BRISKET

SERVES 10
PREP TIME: 30 MINUTES
COOK TIME: 12 TO 14 HOURS

 SUGGESTED WOOD: **Oak or Hickory**

Made famous in many of the city markets around Texas, this is the quintessential Texas smoked brisket recipe. A USDA Prime brisket costs a little more, but the fat content and marbling will be well worth the money. Look for one that is well marbled with a thickness balanced between the flat and the point.

1 (12- to 14-pound) USDA Prime beef brisket

½ cup Dalmatian Rub (page 26)

1 gallon water

1. Trim the exterior fat off the brisket, leaving a fat cap of at least ½ inch thick. Remove any hard pieces of fat and silver skin, as they will not render off during the smoking process.

2. On a baking sheet, generously season the brisket on all sides with the Dalmatian Rub. Return the brisket to the refrigerator while you start your fire.

3. Build a fire using your choice of wood (or a combination of charcoal and wood, depending on the smoker) and bring to 225°F.

4. Pour the water in a foil loaf pan and place it in the smoker as close to the firebox as possible. Place the brisket in the smoker, fat-side up, with the point facing the firebox.

5. Watch the fire closely and maintain a consistent temperature. Check the wood chunks at least once an hour and add more as required, looking for clean, light white smoke. Replenish the water as needed.

6. After about 8 hours, start checking the brisket's temperature with an instant-read thermometer, until it reaches 195°F to 203°F.

7. Remove the brisket from the smoker and double wrap it in heavy duty butcher paper. Place the brisket in a cooler and cover the wrapped brisket with a large towel to help insulate the heat.

8. Allow the brisket to rest for at least 1 hour before slicing, which allows the juices to be absorbed back into the meat.

9. Find where the grain begins to change direction, roughly halfway between the flat and the point, and slice in half widthwise. Starting with the flat, slice the brisket fat-side up and against the grain. Keep your slices to the width of a pencil.

10. Turn the brisket point 90 degrees and slice it in half. Now slice the brisket point against the grain. Serve and enjoy.

Pro Advice: If you are looking for a richer, darker crust, spritz the meat with apple juice or a sugar-based cola every 45 minutes using a compression sprayer. Do not overspray the meat, leaving pools of liquid on the surface.

BEEF PLATE RIBS

SERVES 6
PREP TIME: 30 MINUTES
COOK TIME: 6 TO 7 HOURS

 SUGGESTED WOOD: **Oak or Hickory**

The crown jewel of smoked beef is the plate ribs, affectionately known as "dinosaur ribs" due to their massive size. Plate ribs may be difficult to source in a big-box supermarket, but a visit to your butcher should set you straight.

5 tablespoons kosher salt

2 tablespoons freshly ground black pepper

1 tablespoon granulated garlic

2 (3-bone) beef plate ribs

4 tablespoons yellow mustard

1. In a small bowl, mix the salt, pepper, and granulated garlic together and set aside.

2. If not already trimmed, removed the fat cap and the layer of silver skin from the ribs.

3. Apply 2 tablespoons of the yellow mustard to each of the plate ribs in a thin layer.

4. Generously season the plate ribs with the rub mixture.

5. Build a fire using your choice of wood (or a combination of charcoal and wood, depending on the smoker) and bring it to 300°F. Be sure to check on your wood chunks every 30 minutes and replenish as necessary.

6. Place the ribs in the smoker and cook for about 6 hours, until they reach an internal temperature of 205°F to 210°F using an instant-read thermometer. Check the temperature in multiple places, but be sure not to touch the rib bone with your thermometer to avoid a false reading.

7. Remove the ribs from the smoker, wrap them in butcher paper or foil, and place them in a cooler to rest for 1 hour.

8. Slice the ribs between the bones and enjoy.

WHOLE SMOKED BEEF SHANK

SERVES 6
PREP TIME: 30 MINUTES
COOK TIME: 9 HOURS

 SUGGESTED WOOD: **Mesquite or Hickory**

This tender and delectable shank is first smoked with mesquite, and then finished off with a low braise to break down the collagen in the muscles. When shopping, look for the whole shank, which is also known as the shin or osso buco.

1 (4- to 5-pound) whole beef shank

4 tablespoons Dalmatian Rub (page 26)

2 teaspoons granulated garlic (optional)

2 teaspoons chipotle powder (optional)

1 medium onion, sliced

2 cups beef broth

1. Heat the smoker to 275°F using 4 chunks of mesquite or hickory.

2. Rub the beef shank with the Dalmatian Rub, granulated garlic (if using), and chipotle powder (if using) and place it in the smoker.

3. Smoke the beef for 4 hours, or until it reaches an internal temperature of 155°F.

4. Place the onion and beef broth in a foil pan. Transfer the meat to the foil pan and tightly cover with foil.

5. Return the beef to the smoker and continue to cook another 4 to 5 hours, or until the internal temperature reaches 210°F.

6. Remove the beef from the oven and allow it to rest for 20 minutes.

7. Carefully remove the foil from the pan, avoiding the steam.

8. Using heat-resistant rubber gloves (or 2 forks), pull the beef into 2-inch chunks. Transfer the chunks into a bowl and add some of the remaining braising liquid.

9. If desired, add more Dalmatian Rub, toss, and serve.

PILONCILLO SMOKED CHICKEN

SERVES 6
PREP TIME: 30 MINUTES
MARINATE TIME: 4 HOURS
COOK TIME: 3 HOURS

 SUGGESTED WOOD: **Pecan or Hickory**

Norteño-style cooking from Northern Mexico heavily influenced the food in what's now known as Texas Hill County. This recipe uses chicken along with piloncillo, a Mexican brown sugar usually found in a cone or disc shape, as well as sweet and peppery achiote paste.

1 cup piloncillo sugar, or 1 (8-ounce) solid cone

1 tablespoon achiote paste

1 tablespoon freshly ground black pepper

1 tablespoon kosher salt

2 (3½- to 4-pound) whole chickens

1. Seal the piloncillo in a gallon zip-top bag, removing all of the air from the bag.

2. Using a meat mallet or can, break up the piloncillo until it has the consistency of brown sugar.

3. In a small bowl, combine the piloncillo, achiote paste, pepper, and salt, and mix thoroughly.

4. Spatchcock the chickens (see page 18) and pat them down with paper towels until completely dry.

5. Rub the chickens thoroughly with the piloncillo marinade, making sure to get under the skin, and refrigerate them for 4 hours.

6. Build a fire using 2 chunks of your wood of choice (or a combination of charcoal and wood, depending on the smoker) and bring to 250°F.

7. Place the chickens in the smoker, skin-side down, and cook for 1 hour.

8. Flip the chickens over and place 2 more chunks of wood on the coals. Smoke for 1 hour more, or until the internal temperature reaches 145°F.

9. Loosely place a sheet of heavy-duty foil over the chickens and continue to cook for 1 hour more, until the chicken reaches an internal temperature of 160°F.

10. Remove the chickens from the smoker and allow them to rest for 20 minutes before slicing.

Experiment: For a truly wonderful flavor, brine the chickens in pineapple juice for four hours (or no longer than overnight) prior to rubbing down the chickens with the piloncillo marinade.

PEPPER-CRUSTED TURKEY

SERVES 6
PREP TIME: 30 MINUTES
BRINE TIME: UP TO 24 HOURS
COOK TIME: 7 HOURS

 SUGGESTED WOOD: **Apple mixed with Pecan or Hickory**

The star of the show in Texas is obviously brisket, but this moist and boldly flavored turkey gives it a run for its money. A simple salt and pepper rub is all that is needed to accentuate the richness of the meat.

1 gallon water

2½ cups kosher salt

⅔ cup dark brown sugar

1 tablespoon whole black peppercorns

1 (7-pound) bag ice, divided

1 (14- to 16-pound) whole thawed or fresh turkey

3 tablespoons kosher salt

⅓ cup freshly ground black pepper

2 tablespoons canola or vegetable oil

1. In a large pot over high heat, combine the water, salt, brown sugar, and peppercorns. Bring to a boil and stir for about 3 minutes, until the salt and sugar have dissolved. Remove the brine from the heat and allow it to cool to room temperature for about 1 hour. Stir in ⅓ of the ice into the brine.

2. Place the turkey in a 5-gallon food safe bucket (or brining bag inside a clean bucket). Pour in the brine and the remaining ⅔ of the ice. Seal the bucket and/or bag and refrigerate up to 24 hours.

3. Rinse the turkey under cold water, pat it down completely with paper towels, and place it on a baking sheet. At least 2 hours before smoking, spatchcock the turkey (see page 18).

4. Combine the salt and black pepper in a spice shaker bottle and set aside.

5. Rub the turkey down with the oil, then use the spice shaker to generously cover the turkey with the spice mixture. Place the turkey in the refrigerator, uncovered, for 2 hours.

6. Heat the smoker to 225°F using one chunk each of apple and pecan wood. If using a pellet smoker, pour equal parts of apple and pecan pellets into your hopper and mix thoroughly.

7. Place the turkey in the smoker, skin-side up, and smoke for 3 hours. Replenish the wood chunks each hour.

8. Increase smoker temperature to 325°F and cook for another 3 to 3 ½ hours, or until the internal temperature is 155°F. Loosely drape a sheet of heavy-duty foil over the turkey. Cook for another 30 minutes, or until the turkey reaches an internal temperature of 165°F.

9. Remove the turkey from the smoker and place it on a baking sheet. Allow it to rest for 30 minutes before slicing.

Experiment: For a nice citrus note, quarter and seed two whole oranges and place them in the brine mixture prior to boiling.

PORK SHOULDER STEAKS

SERVES 8 TO 10
PREP TIME: 30 MINUTES
MARINATE TIME: UP TO 8 HOURS
COOK TIME: 6 HOURS

 SUGGESTED WOOD: **Post Oak**

One of the unsung heroes of the Texas barbecue scene is the Pork Shoulder Steak: a whole, bone-in pork shoulder or Boston butt cut into two-inch slices (your butcher can cut it for you). This recipe uses a mop, which is a thin liquid that is brushed (or "mopped") over the meat to keep the surface moist.

1 whole, bone-in pork shoulder, cut into 2-inch steaks

½ cup Dalmatian Rub (page 26)

½ gallon water

1 large white onion, diced

1 stick unsalted butter

½ cup white vinegar

¼ cup Worcestershire sauce

1 tablespoon dry mustard

1. Up to 8 hours before cooking, rub the pork steaks down with the Dalmatian Rub. Cover and refrigerate.

2. Heat the smoker to 275°F. Place 2 chunks of wood on the coals.

3. In a large pot, bring the water to a boil. Add the onion and continue to boil for 10 minutes. Add the butter, vinegar, Worcestershire sauce, and dry mustard to the pot, reduce the heat to low, and bring the mop to a simmer.

4. Place the pork steaks in the smoker. Mop the steaks liberally every 45 minutes, making sure to replenish the wood as needed.

5. After about 4 hours, check the temperature of the steaks. Once they reach 145°F, flip them over and mop them again.

6. Continue to mop the steaks every 45 minutes, or until they reach an internal temperature of 165°F. The meat should be quite tender with crispy fat on the edges.

7. Remove the steaks from the smoker and allow them to rest for 30 minutes. Slice against the grain and serve.

Pro Advice: After making the mop sauce, leave it on the stove on the lowest heat setting to keep it warm.

LAMB SHOULDER BARBACOA

SERVES 6
PREP TIME: 15 MINUTES
COOK TIME: 6 HOURS

 SUGGESTED WOOD: **Hickory or Oak**

Barbacoa is a traditional dish found in Mexico that involves roasting an entire lamb in a pit dug out of the ground, and then slathering it in adobo sauce and covering it in banana or avocado leaves. This adaptation is made for modern smokers and results in succulent, savory, and smoky lamb.

1 cup water

¼ cup apple cider vinegar

1⅓ tablespoons kosher salt, divided

1 tablespoon freshly ground black pepper

1 tablespoon smoked paprika

1 tablespoon granulated garlic

1 teaspoon Mexican oregano

1 teaspoon ground cumin

1 (5-pound) bone-in lamb shoulder

2 tablespoons yellow mustard

1 large white onion, diced, for serving

½ bunch cilantro, chopped, for serving

Juice of ½ lime, for serving

1. Preheat your smoker to 275°F with 3 chunks of wood. In a compression spray bottle, combine the water and vinegar and set aside.

2. In a spice shaker, combine 1 tablespoon of the salt with the pepper, paprika, granulated garlic, oregano, and cumin, and set aside.

3. Rub the lamb shoulder thoroughly with the mustard and then, using the spice shaker, generously cover the meat with the spice rub.

4. Place the lamb in the smoker and cook for 45 minutes. Open the smoker and lightly spray the meat with the vinegar mixture. Repeat this step every 20 to 30 minutes for the next 4 hours.

5. Using an instant-read thermometer, check the temperature of the meat. Once the lamb has reached at least 165°F, wrap it in heavy-duty foil and return it to the smoker.

6. Continue to cook until the internal temperature has reached 195°F. Remove the lamb from the smoker and allow it to rest for 30 minutes.

Flour tortillas,
for serving

Avocado slices,
for serving

7. While the lamb is resting, combine the white onion, cilantro, the remaining salt, and lime juice in a small bowl.

8. Shred the lamb using heat-resistant rubber gloves or a pair of forks.

9. Serve with warm flour tortillas, avocado slices, and the onion mixture.

Ingredient Tip: Cilantro has a soapy taste to some people. If you are unsure about your barbecue guests' preferences, substitute cilantro with diced mint leaves.

CABRITO MOLE POBLANO

SERVES 6
PREP TIME: 30 MINUTES
COOK TIME: 5 HOURS 30 MINUTES

 SUGGESTED WOOD: **Hickory**

If you think goat, also called cabrito, is too gamey or stringy, this recipe may change your mind. Rich, chocolatey mole mellows out the meat's flavor, while low and slow smoking ensures a tender texture. Unfortunately, this delicious piece of Texas-Mexican heritage is slowly dropping off menus at barbecue joints all over Hill Country, but it's easy to learn how to make it yourself to keep the tradition going.

1 tablespoon kosher salt

1 tablespoon freshly ground black pepper

1 tablespoon dried ancho chili powder

1 tablespoon dried guajillo chili powder

2 teaspoons ground cumin

2 teaspoons dark brown sugar

1 teaspoon Mexican oregano

1 teaspoon unsweetened cocoa powder

1 (5- to 6-pound) goat shoulder

3 tablespoons olive oil

16 ounces lager beer, divided

1. Preheat your smoker to 250°F with 3 chunks of wood.

2. In a small bowl, mix the salt, pepper, ancho chili powder, guajillo chili powder, cumin, brown sugar, oregano, and cocoa powder, and set aside.

3. Thoroughly rub the goat with the olive oil, and liberally coat the meat with the spice rub.

4. Place the cabrito in the smoker and cook for 2 hours, and then add 2 more wood chunks.

5. Cook the meat another 2 hours, or until it reaches an internal temperature of 180°F.

6. Place the goat on a large sheet of heavy-duty foil. Fold up the sides of the foil to create a bowl around the goat, then add 8 ounces of the beer. Wrap the meat tightly with foil and return it to the smoker.

7. Place the onions, jalapeños, and poblano in a foil pan, coat them with the vegetable oil, and place them in the smoker. Pour the remaining 8 ounces of beer into the vegetable pan and stir.

1 tablespoon vegetable or canola oil

4 large white onions, quartered and separated

2 jalapeño peppers, sliced and seeded

1 poblano pepper, roughly chopped

8. Continue to cook for another 1½ hours, until it reaches an internal temperature of 200°F.

9. Remove the meat along with the onion and pepper mix from the smoker, and let them rest for 30 minutes.

10. Remove the goat from the foil and carve the meat from the bone. Chop the goat into bite-size pieces and enjoy with the smoked peppers and onions.

Pro Advice: This dish is traditionally cooked directly over coals, allowing the dripping fat smoke to rise back up and flavor the meat. If you have a bullet or kamado smoker, remove the water pan or heat shield for similar results.

CHOPPED BEEF SANDWICHES

SERVES 10
PREP TIME: 30 MINUTES
COOK TIME: 6 HOURS

 SUGGESTED WOOD: **Mesquite or Oak**

Before the prevalence of brisket in Texas barbecue, the beef shoulder reigned supreme. It was especially popular in hearty chopped beef sandwiches served on hamburger buns.

⅓ cup Dalmatian Rub (page 26)

2 teaspoons granulated garlic

2 teaspoons ground cumin

2 teaspoons ground coriander

1 teaspoon cayenne pepper

1 (6-pound) beef shoulder roast or chuck roast

3 tablespoons yellow mustard

¼ cup apple cider vinegar

¼ cup lemon juice

10 potato hamburger buns

Dill pickles, sliced, for serving

2 white or yellow onions, diced, for serving

1. Mix the Dalmatian Rub, granulated garlic, cumin, coriander, and cayenne pepper together in a small spice shaker. Rub the meat down with the yellow mustard thoroughly. Shake the spice rub liberally over the meat until covered and bring to room temperature.

2. Build a fire using your choice of wood. When the smoker reaches 275°F, place the meat on the grate and cook for 3 hours.

3. Remove the meat from the smoker. Double wrap it in heavy-duty foil, making sure no juices can escape, and return it to the smoker for 3 hours more, or until the internal temperature reaches 200°F.

4. Remove the meat from the smoker and allow it to rest for 30 minutes.

5. Unwrap the meat and pour all the drippings into a saucepot. Bring to a simmer. Add the vinegar and lemon juice.

6. Chop the meat, discarding any fat, and mix the dripping sauce back into the meat.

7. Serve on potato buns with pickles and diced onions.

BEEF CHEEK BARBACOA TACOS

SERVES 8
PREP TIME: 20 MINUTES
COOK TIME: 6 TO 7 HOURS

 SUGGESTED WOOD: **Oak**

The beef cheeks in these tacos are smoked, and then slow braised until they are super tender. When you order them at the butcher, ask to have the silver skin removed. Otherwise, you'll need to buy more meat.

¼ cup freshly ground black pepper

2 tablespoons kosher salt, plus 1 teaspoon (*2 tablespoons used first, then 1 teaspoon used later*)

1 tablespoon chipotle powder

1 tablespoon granulated garlic

1 tablespoon ground cumin

3 pounds beef cheeks, trimmed

2 cups low sodium beef broth

16 ounces lager beer

1 medium onion, coarsely chopped

6 garlic cloves, chopped

1 large white onion, diced

1. In a small bowl, mix together the pepper, 2 tablespoons of salt, chipotle powder, granulated garlic, and cumin, and set aside.

2. Season the beef cheeks thoroughly with the rub. Place the cheeks in the refrigerator while you prep the smoker.

3. Build a fire using charcoal along with 2 chunks of wood and bring it to 275°F.

4. Place the cheeks on the grill and smoke for 2 to 2½ hours, or until the internal temperature reaches at least 160°F.

5. Place the broth, beer, medium onion, and garlic cloves in a foil pan.

6. Add the beef cheeks to the braising liquid in the pan and return it to the smoker for another 4 to 5 hours, flipping them over once about halfway through the cook, until tender. Be sure to check your wood chunks each hour and replenish as needed. When the internal temperature reaches 195°F, remove the beef cheeks from the smoker.

½ bunch cilantro, diced

Juice of ½ lime

Small corn tortillas

Cotija cheese

7. Allow the meat to rest for 30 minutes. While the cheeks are resting, combine the large onion, cilantro, remaining teaspoon of salt, and lime juice in a small bowl.

8. Remove the meat from the braising liquid and shred it, adding some of the braising liquid for maximum moisture.

9. Serve on corn tortillas with the onion and cilantro mixture and topped with Cotija cheese.

Pro Advice: If you need to speed up the cook (and don't care as much about smoky flavor), cover the pan with foil when you place the cheeks in the braising liquid.

Four

Kansas City

The Story

In the 1860s, Kansas City, Missouri, lobbied the federal government to make the city a stop on the planned transcontinental railroad. This created a regional hub for commerce and brought in the first meatpacking companies. After the Civil War, beef began flooding into the city. With access to all of these products, a diverse food scene flourished, culminating in The Grand Barbecue of 1880, when more than 3,000 locals were fed.

Fast forward to the 1920s and '30s. Barbecue was in full swing during the jazz renaissance, led by great pitmasters like Henry Perry, the Bryant Brothers, and George Gates. It is rumored that traveling baseball teams and sportscasters fell in love with the 'cue and spread the word throughout the rest of the country.

Best-Kept Secrets

» Many of the recipes in this chapter call for apple cider vinegar. I recommend a raw unfiltered vinegar, which has a sharper taste and stronger apple flavor.

» The same goes for apple juice, as the flavor of the unfiltered variety is more intense.

» Many people mistakenly believe that the perfect rib should fall off the bone. But if that's the case, it has been overcooked. A rib is done when it has what is called "bite through," which means that you can take a bite of the meat and it will come cleanly off the bone with little resistance and without taking any additional meat with it. Be mindful of your temperatures and you will nail this every time.

Classic Sides

Kansas City prides itself on double cooked French fries with a soft center and crisp exterior. Barbecue joints across the state try to outdo each other with their fry rub, which typically features salt, sugar, garlic, onion, and other spices.

Hickory Pit Beans (page 64) are cooked low and slow in the smoker for a deep flavor. Many barbecue joints will add in leftover brisket, pulled pork, or bacon. As much time and effort goes into making the perfect baked bean as the main dish.

Another favorite in Kansas City is mayonnaise-based coleslaw with a bit of vinegar to give it that distinctive twang. A number of restaurants make a spicy version of this slaw with a vinegar-based hot sauce. Unlike other regions, cole-slaw in Kansas City is served on the side and never on the sandwich.

KC BARBECUE RUB

MAKES 5 CUPS
PREP TIME: 5 MINUTES

This Kansas City–style rub is fairly universal, but it works especially well on chicken and pork. It's a version of the barbecue rub that helped kick off our spice rub company over 10 years ago. Sweet paprika combines with a little bit of the smokiness from the chili powder. Unlike white sugar, turbinado sugar will not burn and cause your meat to turn bitter, which means this rub can be used in both low and slow and hot and fast cooking.

1½ cups sweet (or smoked) paprika

1¼ cups turbinado sugar

⅔ cup freshly ground black pepper

⅔ cup kosher salt

⅓ cup chili powder

⅓ cup garlic powder

⅓ cup onion powder

1 tablespoon cayenne powder

1. In a medium bowl, combine all of the ingredients and mix thoroughly.

2. Store the rub in a cool, dark place in a sealable plastic or glass container for no more than 3 months. Spices will oxidize over time and will lose their flavor if stored too long.

Ingredient Tip: For a variation that is better suited for beef, use smoked paprika, which pairs well with the fatty crust that forms.

KC BARBECUE SAUCE

MAKES 3¼ CUPS
PREP TIME: 10 MINUTES
COOK TIME: 1 HOUR 10 MINUTES

 SUGGESTED WOOD: **Hickory**

Once you try this authentic version of Kansas City's sweet, thick, and tangy barbecue sauce, you will never use the store-bought version again. Smoking it adds a depth of flavor that cannot be replicated using liquid smoke alone.

2 tablespoons
salted butter

1 small white onion, diced

2 cups ketchup

⅓ cup dark brown sugar

⅓ cup molasses

¼ cup apple
cider vinegar

1 tablespoon
yellow mustard

1 tablespoon
granulated garlic

1 tablespoon chili powder

1 teaspoon freshly
ground black pepper

½ teaspoon
cayenne pepper

1. Preheat your smoker to 250°F with 3 chunks of wood.

2. In a medium, ovenproof saucepan over medium heat, melt the butter.

3. Add the onion and cook for about 5 minutes, stirring occasionally, until translucent.

4. Add the ketchup, brown sugar, molasses, vinegar, mustard, granulated garlic, chili powder, black pepper, and cayenne pepper, and stir. Allow the sauce to come up to a boil, then reduce to a simmer.

5. Transfer the saucepan to the smoker and smoke for 1 hour, stirring every 10 minutes.

6. Remove the saucepan from the smoker and allow it to rest for 30 minutes.

7. Pour the sauce into a blender and pulse until the sauce has a smooth consistency.

8. Transfer the sauce to a mason jar or airtight container. If stored in the refrigerator, this sauce will keep for 2 weeks.

Pro Advice: If you don't have time to smoke, add ½ teaspoon of liquid smoke, reduce the heat to medium-low, and simmer for 20 to 30 minutes, stirring every 5 minutes.

BURNT ENDS

SERVES 10
PREP TIME: 30 MINUTES
COOK TIME: 12 HOURS

 SUGGESTED WOOD: **Hickory and Cherry**

The quintessential barbecue dish of Kansas City is made from the rendered chunks of the point end of the brisket. After smoking, they're sauced and cooked again until sticky and smoky, and if made properly, they should practically melt in your mouth.

1 (6- to 7-pound) brisket point

2 tablespoons freshly ground black pepper

2 tablespoons kosher salt

2 teaspoons granulated garlic

1 cup beef stock

1 cup KC Barbecue Sauce (page 51)

½ cup dark brown sugar

Sliced white bread, for serving

Dill pickle chips, for serving

1. Trim the brisket point of any loose or hard white fat, and trim the fat cap down to between ¼- and ½-inch thickness.

2. Preheat the smoker to 250°F with 2 chunks of hickory and 2 chunks of cherry wood.

3. In a small bowl, mix the pepper, salt, and granulated garlic. Liberally rub the mixture over all of the brisket.

4. Add the beef stock to a compression sprayer.

5. Place the brisket in the smoker and cook for 6 to 8 hours, or until it reaches an internal temperature of 165°F. Spritz the meat every hour during this step with the beef stock. Be sure to replenish the wood chunks as necessary.

6. Once the brisket reaches 165°F, double wrap the brisket in heavy-duty foil. Return it to the smoker and cook for another 2 to 3 hours, until it reaches an internal temperature of 190°F. Remove the brisket from the smoker and place it on a cutting board.

7. Unwrap the brisket from the foil, draining the liquid into an aluminum pan. Cut the brisket into 1½-inch cubes and place them into the same pan. Add the barbecue sauce and brown sugar, and toss.

8. Return the pan to the smoker uncovered and continue to cook for another 1 to 2 hours, until the burnt ends have absorbed the barbecue sauce but are still tender.

9. Remove the pan from the smoker and serve immediately along with sliced white bread and dill pickle chips.

Pro Advice: You can substitute the use of foil in step 6 with butcher paper. The paper will help preserve the brisket bark better than foil, but expect to lose some of the liquid.

KC BRISKET

SERVES 14
PREP TIME: 30 MINUTES
COOK TIME: 8 TO 10 HOURS

 SUGGESTED WOOD: **Hickory and Oak**

The apple juice and vinegar spritz in this recipe will create a beautiful bark on the meat, while the rub gives it that unique Kansas City flavor.

1 (6- to 7-pound) brisket flat

¾ cup KC Barbecue Rub (page 50)

½ cup apple juice

½ cup apple cider vinegar

1 quart water, heated

1 cup KC Barbecue Sauce (page 51), for serving

1. Preheat your smoker to 250°F with 2 chunks of hickory and 2 chunks of oak wood.

2. Using a sharp knife, trim the fat from the brisket, leaving between ¼ and ½ inch of fat.

3. Place the brisket on an edged baking tray and apply ¼ cup of the rub. Flip the meat over and apply ¼ cup of rub on the other side. Using your hands, apply the remaining rub to the sides of the brisket.

4. In a compression sprayer, mix the apple juice and vinegar, and prime.

5. Pour the water into a metal bowl or aluminum pan and place it in the smoker close to the heat source.

6. Place the brisket in the smoker, fat-side up, and smoke for 1 hour.

7. Spritz the meat with the apple juice mixture. Smoke for another 2 hours, spritzing the meat every 30 minutes. Replenish the wood chunks as needed.

8. Flip the brisket over and smoke for another 3 hours while being sure to spritz the meat every 30 minutes. Replenish the water in the bowl and wood chunks as needed.

9. When the brisket's internal temperature has reached 160°F, wrap it tightly in heavy-duty foil, crimping the edges to ensure a tight seal.

10. Return the brisket to the smoker and cook for 2 to 3 hours more, until it reaches an internal temperature of 195°F.

11. Transfer the brisket to an insulated cooler and allow it to rest for 1 hour.

12. Unwrap the brisket over an edged baking sheet to collect the juices. Slice the brisket thinner than the width of a pencil and place it back in the meat juices. Serve with the barbecue sauce.

BARBECUE MEATLOAF

SERVES 6
PREP TIME: 1 HOUR 30 MINUTES
COOK TIME: 4 HOURS

 SUGGESTED WOOD: **Hickory**

Forget about dry, flavorless meatloaf. A combination of ground 80/20 beef chuck with pork adds the proper amount of fat and savoriness, while hickory wood provides just the right kiss of smoke. You can experiment with different chip flavors.

1 tablespoon canola or vegetable oil

1 medium white onion, diced

3 garlic cloves, minced

1 (8-ounce) bag barbecue-flavored potato chips

¾ cup ketchup

¼ cup tomato paste

2 tablespoons brown sugar

1 tablespoon Worcestershire sauce

2 pounds 80/20 ground beef chuck

1 pound ground pork

2 tablespoons KC Barbecue Rub (page 50)

1. Heat the oil in a small pan over medium heat. Add the onion and cook until translucent. Add the garlic, stirring constantly, and cook for another 2 minutes. Remove from the heat and set aside.

2. Crush the potato chips in the bag until they resemble breadcrumbs.

3. In a small bowl, combine the onion mixture, ketchup, tomato paste, brown sugar, and Worcestershire sauce. Set aside ¼ cup of this mixture.

4. In a large bowl, add the ground beef, ground pork, potato chips, barbecue rub, and sauce and mix until thoroughly incorporated. On a foil-lined baking sheet, form the meat into a 12-inch loaf. Cover and refrigerate for 1 hour.

5. Preheat your smoker to 250°F with 3 chunks of wood.

6. Using the foil, turn the loaf out onto the smoker. Brush the remaining sauce onto the meatloaf. Smoke for 4 hours, or until it reaches an internal temperature of 160°F.

7. Transfer the meatloaf from the smoker onto a baking sheet and allow to rest for 20 minutes. Slice and serve.

PORK BELLY BURNT ENDS

SERVES 10
PREP TIME: 30 MINUTES
MARINATE TIME: 2 TO 8 HOURS
COOK TIME: 4 HOURS

 SUGGESTED WOOD: **Cherry or Hickory**

This Burnt End variation has gained popularity in recent years using the best part of the pig—the belly, where bacon comes from. These are incredibly tender and full of flavor, and they will practically melt in your mouth. Once you sink your teeth into these candied and salty pig morsels, you will be hooked.

For the rub

½ cup turbinado or raw sugar

¼ cup sweet paprika

2 tablespoons kosher salt

1 tablespoon light chili powder

1 tablespoon granulated garlic

1 tablespoon granulated onion

1½ teaspoons freshly ground black pepper

1 teaspoon cayenne pepper

For the meat

1 (4- to 5-pound) pork belly, skin removed

1 cup KC Barbecue Sauce (page 51)

1 tablespoon honey

½ cup low sodium chicken stock

1. **To make the rub:** In a medium bowl, mix all of the rub ingredients together and set aside.

2. **To make the meat:** Cut the pork belly into 2-inch cubes. Season the cubes thoroughly with the rub, then cover and store them the refrigerator overnight (or for at least 2 hours).

3. Build a fire using your choice of wood (or a combination of charcoal and wood, depending on the smoker) and bring it to 250°F.

4. Space out the belly cubes on a non-coated wire rack. Place the rack in the smoker and cook for 2 hours.

5. In a small bowl, mix the barbecue sauce, honey, and chicken stock. Remove the cubes from the smoker and transfer them to a disposable foil pan in a single layer. Pour the sauce mixture over the cubes and toss until well coated. Cover the pan with foil and return it to the smoker for another 1½ hours.

6. Remove the foil, toss the cubes carefully again in the sauce, then cook for an additional 30 minutes, until the pork is sticky and thick.

PORK SPARERIBS 3-2-1

SERVES 6
PREP TIME: 30 MINUTES
COOK TIME: 6 HOURS

 SUGGESTED WOOD: **Cherry**

When smoking spareribs, I have found that the tried and true 3-2-1 method works the best. This means three hours of smoke, two hours in foil, and one hour of saucing, resulting in perfect ribs every time.

⅓ cup dark brown sugar

1 tablespoon kosher salt

1 tablespoon freshly ground black pepper

2 teaspoons smoked paprika

1 teaspoon granulated garlic

1 teaspoon granulated onion

1 teaspoon mustard powder

1 teaspoon celery salt

½ teaspoon cayenne pepper

1 cup apple juice

2 racks pork spareribs

6 tablespoons salted butter, sliced into pats

4 tablespoons honey

½ cup KC Barbecue Sauce (page 51)

1. Preheat your smoker to 225°F with 3 chunks of wood.

2. In a small bowl, mix the brown sugar, kosher salt, black pepper, paprika, granulated garlic, granulated onion, mustard powder, celery salt, and cayenne pepper, and set aside. Pour the apple juice into a compression sprayer.

3. Remove the membrane off the back of the ribs. Liberally season both sides of the ribs with the dry rub, starting on the bone side.

4. Place the ribs in the smoker and cook for 3 hours, spritzing the ribs with the apple juice every hour.

5. Remove the ribs from the smoker and place each rack on a sheet of heavy-duty foil long enough to cover the ribs. Place 3 pats of butter on each of the racks, along with 2 tablespoons of honey, and about 2 tablespoons of apple juice from the spritzer.

6. Crimp the foil tightly and return them to the smoker. Cook for an additional 2 hours.

7. Carefully remove the ribs from the smoker and place them on a cutting board. Using tongs, remove the ribs from the foil, being careful of the hot steam, and return them to the smoker.

8. Add another chunk of wood to the fire. Rub the meat down with the barbecue sauce and smoke for 1 hour more, or until the ribs are done to your desired tenderness. The ribs should be between 195°F to 205°F. Let the ribs rest for 20 minutes, then slice and enjoy.

Pro Advice: I like to separate the rib tips from the ribs when they are done and keep them for later, as they are an amazing addition to baked beans or chili. I find it easier to separate the bones and cartilage from the meat while it's still hot and before it congeals.

STICKY BABY BACK RIBS

SERVES 6

PREP TIME: 20 MINUTES

MARINATE TIME: 8 HOURS

COOK TIME: 6 HOURS

 SUGGESTED WOOD: **Hickory and Cherry**

Baby back ribs tend to be leaner and more tender than other ribs. An apple juice–based spritz helps keep the meat moist, allows for the smoke to penetrate the meat, and helps form a beautiful crust.

3 (6-pound) racks baby back ribs

1 cup KC Barbecue Rub (page 50)

2 cups apple juice

1 cup apple cider vinegar

2 cups KC Barbecue Sauce (page 51)

1. Rinse the ribs under cold water to remove any bone chips. If the membrane is still intact, insert a butter knife under it and loosen. Using a paper towel, grip the membrane and peel it off.

2. Place the ribs on an edged sheet tray, meat-side down, and rub down the bone side of the meat with about 2 tablespoons of the rub on each rack. Flip the ribs over and repeat the process on the meat side. Cover the ribs with foil or food wrap and place them in the refrigerator overnight.

3. Preheat your smoker to 225°F with 2 chunks of hickory and 1 chunk of cherry wood.

4. In a compression sprayer, mix the apple juice and vinegar together.

5. Place the ribs on the grill and smoke for 5 to 6 hours, spritzing them with the apple juice mixture every 30 minutes. After 2 hours, add 1 more hickory wood chunk and 1 more cherry wood chunk.

6. Cook the ribs until they reach an internal temperature of 180°F. Mop on the barbecue sauce and cook for another 20 minutes, then mop the ribs again. Cook for 20 minutes more, or until the internal temperature reaches 200°F.

7. Remove the ribs from the smoker and allow them to rest for 20 minutes. Slice and enjoy with the remaining sauce as an optional dip, if desired.

Ingredient Tip: If you like your ribs a little sweeter, when applying the rub to the ribs, add 2 tablespoons of brown sugar to each rib on the meat side prior to placing them in the refrigerator. If you use light brown sugar, the ribs will have a sweeter flavor, or try dark brown sugar for more of a molasses taste.

BARBECUE BOURBON CHICKEN

SERVES 6
PREP TIME: 20 MINUTES
MARINATE TIME: 8 TO 12 HOURS
COOK TIME: 2 HOURS 30 MINUTES

 SUGGESTED WOOD: **Apple or Hickory**

This is one of my favorite ways to make chicken. It's smoky and sweet thanks to my KC Barbecue Sauce and dark brown sugar, and we bring bourbon to this party. Note that at these cooking temperatures, not all the alcohol will evaporate from the chicken.

For the chicken

2 whole (3- to 3½-pound) fryer chickens

2 tablespoons olive oil

1 tablespoon baking powder

4 tablespoons KC Barbecue Rub (page 50)

For the sauce

1½ cups KC Barbecue Sauce (page 51)

⅓ cup bourbon

3 tablespoons dark brown sugar

2 tablespoons hot sauce

1 tablespoon canola or vegetable oil

1 tablespoon yellow mustard

1½ teaspoons granulated garlic

1. **To make the chicken:** Preheat your smoker to 275°F with 2 chunks of applewood.

2. Spatchcock your chicken (see page 18). Using a boning knife, cut the chicken in half between the breasts. You should now have 4 chicken halves.

3. Rub the skin down evenly with the olive oil. Sprinkle the baking powder and rub all over the chicken liberally on both sides.

4. **To make the sauce:** In a small bowl, whisk all of the sauce ingredients together, and set aside.

5. Place the chicken in the smoker and cook for about 1½ hours, or until the internal temperature reaches 145°F.

6. Baste the chicken with the sauce every 15 minutes for 1 hour, until the chicken reaches an internal temperature of 165°F. Remove the chicken from the smoker and allow it to rest for 10 minutes before slicing and serving.

Pro Advice: Adding olive oil to the skin keeps it from getting rubbery or soggy.

Hickory Pit Beans

RECIPE ON NEXT PAGE

HICKORY PIT BEANS

SERVES 16
PREP TIME: 30 MINUTES
SOAK TIME: OVERNIGHT
COOK TIME: 6 HOURS 30 MINUTES

 SUGGESTED WOOD: **Hickory**

These old-school beans are sweet, smoky, and meaty, thanks to the addition of everyone's favorite pork cut: bacon. Go ahead and make your grandma proud with from-scratch beans, which have a meatier texture than canned.

2 pounds white navy or great northern beans

2 teaspoons kosher salt

8 slices bacon

1 sweet onion, diced

1 red bell pepper, diced

1 garlic clove, minced

2 cups KC Barbecue Sauce (page 51)

¼ cup light brown sugar

¼ cup Dijon mustard

¼ cup jalapeño peppers, diced

2 tablespoons KC Barbecue Rub (page 50)

1 tablespoon molasses

1. Place the beans and salt in a large saucepan, cover with water by 2 to 3 inches, and soak overnight.

2. Drain and rinse the beans. Return the beans to the large saucepan and cover with 4 inches fresh water. Bring to a boil, then lower the heat and simmer for 1½ hours, until the beans are tender but not bursting open.

3. Preheat your smoker to 250°F with 2 chunks of wood.

4. In a pan over medium heat, cook the bacon until it is almost crisp. Remove the bacon from the pan and dab the slices with paper towels. Reserve about 1 tablespoon of bacon grease in the pan, discarding the rest, then roughly chop the cooked bacon.

5. Add the onion and bell pepper to the reserved bacon grease and cook on medium heat until translucent. Add the garlic, stirring constantly, and cook for another 2 minutes.

6. Drain the beans, reserving 2 cups of the bean water. Transfer the beans to a deep, half-size aluminum pan. Stirring the bean mixture thoroughly, add the barbecue sauce, brown sugar, mustard, jalapeño, barbecue rub, and molasses.

7. Place the beans in the smoker and cook for 5 hours, stirring every hour. Replenish the wood chunks as needed. If the beans start to get too thick, add some of the bean water and stir.

8. After 5 hours, the beans should look dark and sticky and will be tender, with a slightly creamy texture. Remove the beans from the smoker and serve.

Pro Advice: To get some next-level flavor, place the pan of beans underneath a cooking pork butt or brisket to allow the meat drippings to flavor the beans. Be sure that the pork or brisket is over 145°F to ensure that no undercooked meat drippings are getting into your beans.

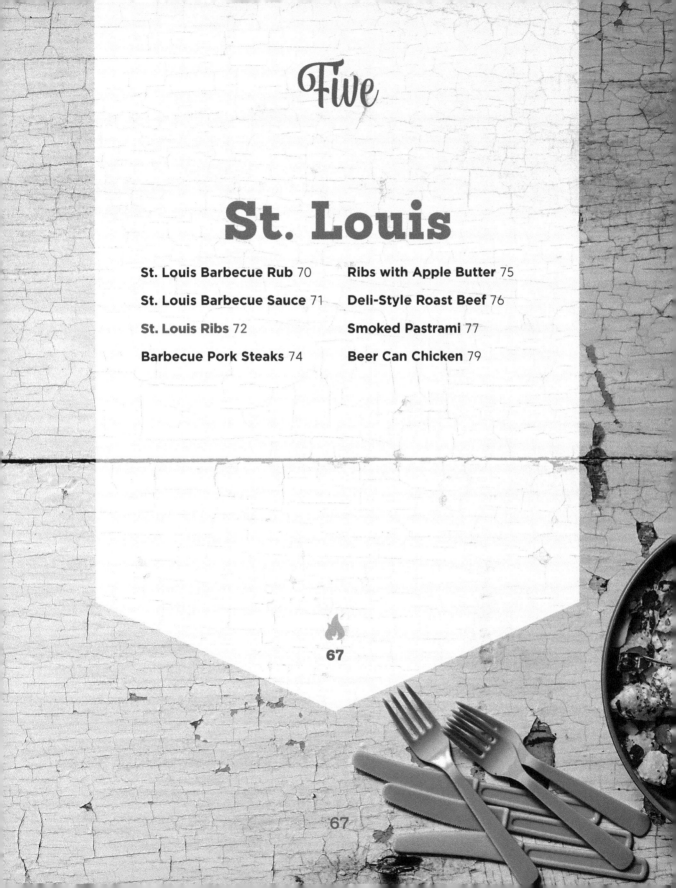

Five

St. Louis

67

The Story

Known as the "Gateway to the West," St. Louis, Missouri, is also where the North meets the South. Due to its history as a major trade route on the Mississippi River, the city has had access to flavors from all over the South. St. Louis's sweet, tomato-based concoction is similar to Kansas City's, but adds vinegar. The region welcomes pork, beef, and poultry equally to its grills.

Best-Kept Secrets

» Many of the recipes in this section call for dark brown sugar instead of light brown sugar. Dark brown sugar contains more molasses and has a richer flavor. If you find yourself with no brown sugar on hand, have no fear. Combine one tablespoon of molasses with white granulated sugar in a food processor and pulse until fully incorporated to create something equivalent to light brown sugar. Use two tablespoons of molasses to create dark brown sugar.

» "It ain't cookin' if you're lookin'." Opening the lid to the smoker to take a selfie lets out valuable heat and moisture, which will add to your cooking time. Get someone to take a photo for you as you're working to minimize the time that the lid is open.

Side Dishes

The folks in St. Louis love their macaroni and cheese so much they now hold an annual festival and competition called the Mac 'N' Cheese Throwdown. While most entries come topped with a toasted cracker or breadcrumb crust, many of the popular 'cue joints have upped their game with more adventurous add-ons, such as pork belly and lobster.

St. Louis is a big potato salad town. Its classic version is made with generous amounts of mayonnaise, though some would argue that Miracle Whip is the way to go. A much adored rendition—my favorite, in fact—uses a generous amount of chopped hardboiled eggs along with traditional celery and onions.

Gooey butter cake has to be one of the best things I've ever eaten in St. Louis. Essentially coffee cake with a sweet custard top and a dusting of powdered sugar, this dessert is served all over the region.

ST. LOUIS BARBECUE RUB

MAKES 3 CUPS
PREP TIME: 5 MINUTES

This sweet and savory rub is ideal for pork ribs and shoulders, especially when paired with the vinegary St. Louis Barbecue Sauce (page 71). It pairs the sweetness of brown sugar with the savory notes of oregano and coriander.

1 cup light brown sugar

½ cup kosher salt

½ cup smoked paprika

¼ cup dry mustard

¼ cup granulated garlic

¼ cup granulated onion

2 tablespoons dried oregano

2½ tablespoons freshly ground black pepper

1 tablespoon ground coriander

2 teaspoons cayenne pepper

1 teaspoon fennel seeds (optional)

1 teaspoon cumin seeds (optional)

1. In a medium bowl, combine all of the ingredients and mix thoroughly.

2. Store the rub in a cool, dark place in a sealable plastic or glass container for no more than 3 months. Spices will oxidize over time and will lose their flavor if stored for too long.

Experiment: If you like your ribs more savory, I suggest adding in the optional fennel and cumin seeds to the rub. The fennel seeds will provide a licorice taste, while the cumin seeds will add warm and earthy notes to the meat.

ST. LOUIS BARBECUE SAUCE

MAKES 3½ CUPS
PREP TIME: 10 MINUTES
COOK TIME: 20 MINUTES
REST TIME: 20 TO 30 MINUTES (OR UP TO 24 HOURS IN THE REFRIGERATOR)

St. Louis Barbecue Sauce is similar to Kansas City's, but it's thinner due to the Southern-worthy addition of vinegar. This sauce also has a lower sugar content, which means it can be used in both low and slow as well as hot and fast cooking.

2 cups ketchup

½ cup water

½ cup apple cider vinegar

⅓ cup dark brown sugar

2 tablespoons yellow mustard

1 tablespoon granulated onion

1 tablespoon granulated garlic

½ tablespoon cayenne

½ tablespoon kosher salt

1 teaspoon crushed red pepper

1. In a medium saucepan over medium-low heat, combine all of the ingredients.

2. Stirring occasionally to avoid burning, allow the sauce to simmer for 20 minutes.

3. Remove the sauce from the heat and allow it to rest for about 20 to 30 minutes. The sauce should be thin, but not runny.

Pro Advice: You can use this sauce immediately after cooling, but, in my opinion, it tastes better if it rests for a day in the refrigerator, which allows the flavors to fully develop. When ready to use, just reheat it in a saucepan on low heat.

ST. LOUIS RIBS

SERVES 6 TO 8
PREP TIME: 20 MINUTES
COOK TIME: 5 HOURS
REST TIME: 20 MINUTES

 SUGGESTED WOOD: **Cherry or Hickory**

This recipe uses what's known as the St. Louis cut: spareribs trimmed down to remove the rib tips. Found on the belly of the hog, they're meatier and fattier than baby back ribs. They are also flatter in shape, making for a much nicer presentation. The spritzed vinegar and the sauce are St. Louis to the core. In fact, these ribs are the mainstay of the local competitive barbecue circuit.

3 racks St. Louis-cut pork ribs

¼ cup yellow mustard

6 tablespoons St. Louis Barbecue Rub (page 70)

1 cup apple juice

½ cup apple cider vinegar

1 cup St. Louis Barbecue Sauce (page 71)

1. Preheat your smoker to 250°F with 4 chunks of wood.

2. Remove the membrane from the bone side of the ribs and rub them down with the mustard. Sprinkle both sides of the ribs with the barbecue rub.

3. Mix the apple juice and vinegar in a compression sprayer.

4. Place the ribs in the smoker and cook for 4 hours, spritzing them with the juice mixture every 30 minutes. Replenish the wood chunks as needed.

5. Brush the ribs with the barbecue sauce to create a glaze. Apply another coat of sauce after 20 minutes.

6. The ribs will be done when the internal temperature has reached 190°F. Remove them from the smoker and allow them to rest for 20 minutes.

Pro Advice: As an added measure to ensure that the ribs stay moist, place an aluminum pan with water inside the smoker closest to the heat source.

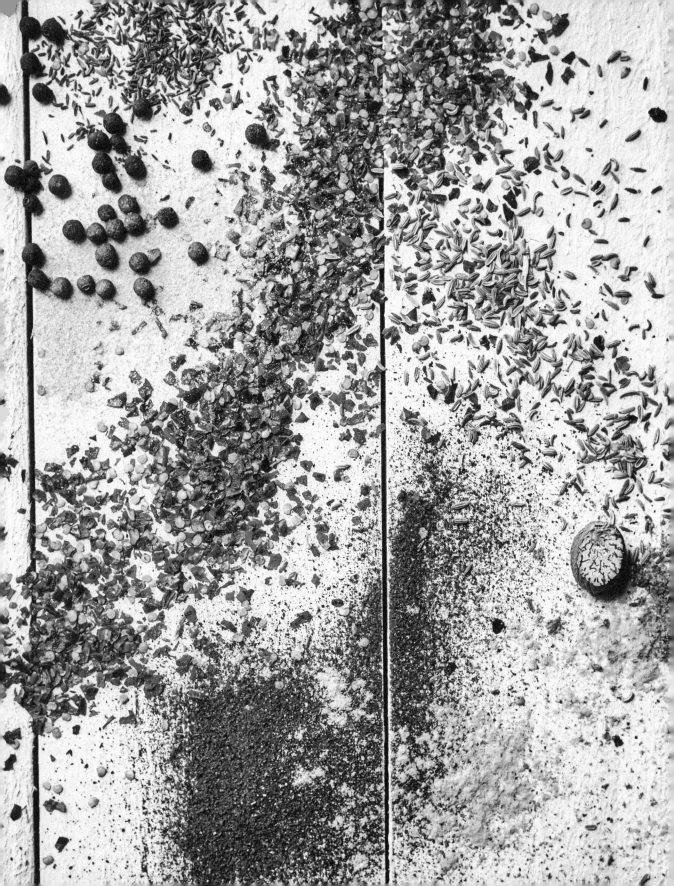

BARBECUE PORK STEAKS

SERVES 6 TO 8
PREP TIME: 1 HOUR 30 MINUTES
COOK TIME: 4 HOURS 30 MINUTES

 SUGGESTED WOOD: **Hickory or Cherry**

Although recipes calling for "pork steaks" date back to the 19th century, the cut gained popularity in the 1950s and became a staple on menus in the 1960s. They're no longer as popular, so they can be difficult to find at big-box stores today, but your local butcher should have them.

For the rub

¼ cup light brown sugar

1 tablespoon cumin

1 tablespoon granulated garlic

1 tablespoon granulated onion

1 tablespoon kosher salt

1 tablespoon smoked paprika

½ tablespoon red pepper flakes

1 teaspoon ground coriander

For the meat

3 (2-inch-thick, 2-pound) pork steaks

2 cups St. Louis Barbecue Sauce (page 71)

1. **To make the rub:** In a small bowl, combine all of the rub ingredients.

2. **To make the meat:** Season the pork steaks generously with the rub and place them in the refrigerator for at least 1 hour.

3. Heat the smoker to 250°F using 2 chunks of wood

4. Place the pork steaks in your smoker and cook for 3 hours.

5. Make the sauce and transfer it to a large disposable aluminum pan.

6. Carefully remove the pork steaks from the smoker and toss them in the sauce. Cover the pan with foil and cook for 1 hour more.

7. Check the steaks and ensure that the sauce is not too thick or dry. If it is, add a small amount of water. Carefully flip the steaks over, cover, and return them to the smoker for an additional 30 minutes.

8. Remove the pan from the smoker, place the steaks on a platter, and serve.

Ingredient Tip: Traditionally, these steaks are cooked over hickory wood, but cherry wood produces a flavor that is light and sweet.

RIBS WITH APPLE BUTTER

SERVES 6 TO 8
PREP TIME: 20 MINUTES
COOK TIME: 6 HOURS

 SUGGESTED WOOD: **Apple**

Reminiscent of pork chops and applesauce, this recipe uses meatier St. Louis–cut spareribs that are infused with the flavor of apple butter. Apple butter, which is actually just a concentrated form of applesauce, can be found in the jam and jelly aisle of most grocery stores or online.

3 racks of St. Louis-cut pork ribs

3 tablespoons apple cider vinegar

1 cup apple butter, divided

6 tablespoons St. Louis Barbecue Rub (page 70)

2 cups St. Louis Barbecue Sauce (page 71)

¼ cup apple juice

1. Preheat your smoker to 250°F with 4 chunks of wood.

2. Remove the membrane from the bone side of the ribs, then rub down each rib with 1 tablespoon of the vinegar. Allow the ribs to rest for about 15 minutes, then slather the ribs with ½ cup of the apple butter, and generously season both sides of the ribs with the rub.

3. Smoke the ribs for about 5 hours. Replenish the wood chunks as needed.

4. In a small saucepan, combine the St. Louis Barbecue Sauce, the remaining ½ cup of apple butter, and the apple juice, then warm the mixture over medium heat for about 5 minutes, until the sauce is fully combined and can cover the back of a spoon.

5. Sauce the ribs and cook for 1 hour more, reapplying the sauce every 20 minutes. The ribs will be done when they have reached an internal temperature of 195°F.

6. Remove the ribs from the smoker and allow them to rest for 20 minutes before slicing.

DELI-STYLE ROAST BEEF

SERVES 6 TO 8
PREP TIME: 30 MINUTES
COOK TIME: 3 HOURS

 SUGGESTED WOOD: **Oak or Hickory**

Made famous by Lion's Choice, a local restaurant chain, this St. Louis staple is iconic. The roast beef is smoked low and slow until warmed through and rare, and then flavored with a slathering of garlic, rosemary, and thyme.

½ cup beef stock

1 teaspoon Worcestershire sauce

1 (3- to 3½-pound) eye of round roast

3 tablespoons minced garlic

2 tablespoons freshly minced rosemary

2 tablespoons freshly minced thyme

2 tablespoons olive oil

1½ tablespoons kosher salt

1½ tablespoons freshly ground black pepper

Sesame buns, for serving

1. Preheat your smoker to 225°F with 2 chunks of wood.

2. Mix the beef stock and Worcestershire sauce, and load the mixture into a meat injector.

3. Trim the excess fat and silver skin from the roast.

4. Insert the injector into the roast and inject the mixture as you pull it out from the meat. Repeat this process in a grid pattern all over the roast. Wipe up any excess liquid from the surface of the roast.

5. Combine the garlic, rosemary, thyme, oil, salt, and pepper, and mix into a paste. Slather the paste all over the surface of the roast.

6. Smoke the roast for about 2½ to 3 hours, or until the internal temperature reaches 125°F.

7. Remove the roast from the smoker and slice it very thin. Serve on lightly toasted and buttered buns.

Pro Advice: Since there won't be any drippings from this recipe, you can make an easy au jus dipping sauce using just two ingredients. In a small saucepan over medium heat, combine two cups of beef broth and two tablespoons of low sodium soy sauce and cook until it comes to a low boil. Turn off the heat and serve.

SMOKED PASTRAMI

SERVES 6 TO 8
PREP TIME: 60 MINUTES
BRINE TIME: 8 DAYS
COOK TIME: 8 HOURS

 SUGGESTED WOOD: **Cherry or Hickory**

Homemade pastrami may seem like quite an endeavor, but this recipe will walk you through all the steps. The recipe uses pink curing salt, also known as Prague Powder #1. It is a curing mixture used on sausages, corned beef, and pastrami, and contains sodium nitrate and table salt. The sodium nitrate will turn the meat pink and helps extend its shelf life.

1 (5- to 6-pound) brisket flat

1 gallon distilled water

¾ cup kosher salt

6 tablespoons pickling spice

2 teaspoons pink curing salt #1 (aka Prague Powder #1)

2 tablespoons freshly ground black pepper

1 tablespoon ground coriander

1 tablespoon granulated garlic

1 tablespoon granulated onion

1 teaspoon mustard powder

1. Trim and discard the excess fat and silver skin from the brisket flat, and place the brisket in a large brining bag.

2. Mix the water, kosher salt, pickling spice, and pink curing salt, and pour the mixture into the brining bag. Remove all the air from the bag and tightly seal and store it in the refrigerator for 7 days, flipping over daily.

3. On the seventh day, remove the brisket from the brining bag and rinse it with cold water. Transfer the brisket into a pot, cover it with cold water, and place it in the refrigerator for 8 hours. This step will remove the excess salt.

4. Preheat your smoker to 225°F with 3 chunks of wood.

5. In a small bowl, mix the pepper, coriander, granulated garlic, granulated onion, and mustard powder together, and set aside.

6. Remove the brisket from the refrigerator and dry it with a paper towel. Sprinkle the rub all over the meat and place it in the smoker for 4 hours. Replenish the wood chunks as needed.

7. Using an instant-read thermometer, when the brisket has reached an internal temperature of 165°F, wrap it tightly in heavy-duty foil. Be sure to crimp the edges well to ensure a tight seal.

8. Return the brisket to the smoker and cook for about 4 hours more, until it reaches an internal temperature of 203°F.

9. Remove the brisket from the smoker and allow it to rest for 1 hour. Remove the brisket from the foil, slice it about ⅛ inch thick, and serve.

Ingredient Tip: If you don't have a spare eight days to make pastrami, you can cheat and pick up a corned beef flat from the grocery store. Start the process on step 3 and desalinate the corned beef. This will remove the excess saltiness and some of the commercial brining solution. Follow the rest of the recipe as shown. If you don't tell anyone, I promise I won't either.

BEER CAN CHICKEN

SERVES 6 TO 8
PREP TIME: 30 MINUTES
COOK TIME: 6 HOURS

 SUGGESTED WOOD: **Hickory or Apple**

Best shared with friends and family, this game day classic is always a winner. The can-stuffed chicken adds to the spectacle—look for all of the *oohs* and *aahs* as you remove the chicken from the smoker.

3 tablespoons dark brown sugar

1 tablespoon chili powder

1 tablespoon kosher salt

1 tablespoon smoked paprika

2 teaspoons granulated garlic

1 teaspoon freshly ground black pepper

1 (4- to 5-pound) whole roaster chicken

2 tablespoons canola or vegetable oil

1 (12-ounce) can of beer, preferably a lager

1. Preheat your smoker to 225°F with 2 chunks of hickory and 1 chunk of applewood.

2. In a small bowl, mix together the brown sugar, chili powder, salt, paprika, granulated garlic, and pepper to create the rub, and set aside.

3. Dry the chicken with a paper towel. Rub down the chicken with the oil, then generously apply the rub to all sides of the chicken.

4. Pour out ¼ of the beer, and then place the chicken's cavity over the top of the can. To increase the stability of the chicken, use a chicken throne (a roasting tool available at most big-box stores or online).

5. Place an aluminum pan with water in the smoker near the heat source.

6. Place the bird in the smoker and cook for 5 to 6 hours, or until an instant-read thermometer reads 165° at the thickest part of the breast and thigh.

7. Remove the meat from the smoker and allow it to rest before slicing and serving.

Ingredient Tip: For a twist, use a can of hard apple cider in place of the beer.

Six

Memphis

Memphis Barbecue Rub 84

Memphis Barbecue Sauce 85

Memphis Pulled Pork 86

Dry Baby Back Ribs 88

Wet Baby Back Ribs 90

Barbecue Cornish Hen 92

Smoked Bologna Chub 94

The Story

Its geographic location in the United States places Memphis between the barbecue styles of Texas, Kansas City, St. Louis, and Alabama, and its versatile style has been influenced by these other regions. As a port city on the Mississippi, Memphis has had easy access to a wide range of spices, including oregano, thyme, and cumin. Memphis is all about pork—especially ribs and shoulders—and its savory rub is what sets it apart from the others.

Best-Kept Secrets

» In this chapter, baby back ribs feature in two different recipes. The removal of the membrane on the back of the ribs is critical to successful cooking. Place the ribs with the bones facing upward on a cutting board, insert a butter knife between the membrane and the bone, and gently loosen the membrane. Work your fingers into the gap to further loosen the membrane. Using a paper towel, grab the membrane and gently peel it off. For more professional-looking ribs, remove the flap of meat from the diaphragm that is covering some of the ribs.

» Nearly every recipe in this chapter uses yellow mustard as a binder. Very little of the mustard flavor comes through in the final product. Do not be concerned if you do not have any yellow mustard on hand when it is time to cook. You can easily substitute any vinegar-based hot sauce or a neutral oil, such as canola or vegetable, as the binder.

» I typically use the sweet or American paprika for these recipes, but if you want to experiment, try smoked paprika. Or substitute some of the paprika with either ancho or chipotle pepper powder to add some heat.

Classic Sides

A uniquely Memphis side dish, barbecue spaghetti is made by simmering cooked spaghetti, Memphis Barbecue Sauce (page 85), and leftover pork rib meat or pulled pork together for about 15 minutes, until fully incorporated. Some barbecue joints make a hybrid dish and add tomato sauce to the combination to add acidity and an Italian flair. It may sound unusual, but give it a try.

Another Memphis staple side is mustard-based coleslaw made with smaller pieces of cabbage. It gets an added twang from vinegar or sometimes even hot sauce. It's also used as a topping on pulled pork sandwiches.

Barbecue beans are also found in just about every Memphis 'cue joint. The recipes vary widely, but many include cuts of pork and tangy barbecue sauce and are typically smoked out on the pit. The beans tend to be hearty and smoky, picking up flavor from cooking for hours on the pits. For added flavor, bits of pork fat are added to the mixture and allowed to render down, even further releasing their flavor into the beans.

MEMPHIS BARBECUE RUB

MAKES 2 CUPS
PREP TIME: 5 MINUTES

Memphis has a long history as a port city on the Mississippi. This gave them access to spices that much of America didn't have. Memphis's standard barbecue rub, used on its famous dry-rubbed ribs, is dominated by spices like oregano, thyme, and cumin, which are not typically found in the barbecue styles of other regions. Unlike other barbecue rubs, this one has no sugar in it.

½ cup sweet paprika

3 tablespoons chili powder

3 tablespoons kosher salt

3 tablespoons freshly ground black pepper

2 tablespoons granulated garlic

2 tablespoons granulated onion

2 tablespoons celery seed

1 tablespoon dried oregano

1 tablespoon dried thyme

1 tablespoon ground cumin

1 tablespoon dry mustard

2 teaspoons ground coriander

1 teaspoon cayenne

1 teaspoon Ac'cent flavor enhancer or MSG (optional)

1. In a small bowl, combine all of the ingredients and mix thoroughly.

2. Store the rub in a cool, dark place in a sealable plastic or glass container for no more than 3 months. Spices will oxidize over time and will lose their flavor if stored for too long.

Ingredient Tip: A flavor enhancer made from Monosodium Glutamate (MSG), Ac'cent can be readily found in grocery stores. While some people don't react well to it, there has been a significant amount of research showing that, in small amounts, MSG is harmless to most people.

MEMPHIS BARBECUE SAUCE

MAKES 3 CUPS
PREP TIME: 5 MINUTES
COOK TIME: 1 HOUR

Many in Memphis say the only way to eat ribs is dry, or without sauce, but for those who are fans of the wet style, this sweet and tangy sauce pairs well with the Memphis rub, creating a perfect balance of flavors. It's also featured in the Memphis Pulled Pork (page 86) and Wet Baby Back Ribs (page 90) recipes. See the tip for a great variation on this recipe.

2 cups ketchup

1 cup water

1 cup peach juice (optional, see tip)

½ cup apple cider vinegar

¼ cup dark brown sugar

¼ cup granulated white sugar

2 tablespoons lemon juice

2 tablespoons Worcestershire sauce

1 tablespoon Memphis Barbecue Rub (page 84)

1½ teaspoons freshly ground black pepper

1½ teaspoons granulated onion

1½ teaspoons mustard powder

1. In a medium saucepot over medium-high heat, combine all of the ingredients and bring them to a boil, stirring frequently to prevent sticking and burning.

2. Reduce the temperature to low and simmer, uncovered, for 1 hour, stirring occasionally.

3. Remove the sauce from the heat and allow it to cool.

4. If stored in a tightly sealed container, this sauce will keep in the refrigerator for up to 1 month.

Experiment: For a totally different twist on this recipe, substitute the water with fresh local peach juice. The Memphis region has been famous for its peach orchards for generations, and this variation pays homage to that heritage. When reduced, the sauce will caramelize and intensify the peach flavor. Give this variation a try and see who can figure out the secret ingredient.

MEMPHIS PULLED PORK

SERVES 12
PREP TIME: 15 MINUTES
COOK TIME: 10 TO 12 HOURS

 SUGGESTED WOOD: **Cherry and Hickory**

Memphis barbecue is all about low and slow cooked pork. This recipe features long strands of pulled pork, prepared with classic Memphis Barbecue Rub and smothered in sweet and tangy Memphis Barbecue Sauce. When shopping, look for a seven- to eight-pound shoulder, as they're typically well marbled and can hold up to long cooks.

1 (7- to 8-pound) pork shoulder

3 tablespoons yellow mustard

¼ cup Memphis Barbecue Rub (page 84)

½ cup apple juice

Memphis Barbecue Sauce (page 85), for serving

1. Preheat your smoker to 225°F with 2 chunks of cherry and 1 chunk of hickory wood.

2. Lightly trim the pork shoulder of any loose fat, being sure to leave the fat cap intact.

3. Thoroughly rub the pork shoulder with the mustard and barbecue rub.

4. Place an aluminum pan with water close to the heat source. Place the pork in the smoker, fat-side up.

5. Cook the pork for about 8 hours, until it reaches an internal temperature of 180°F, replenishing the water and wood as needed.

6. Lay out a double-thick layer of foil and put the pork shoulder in the middle. Fold up the sides of the foil to create a bowl around the shoulder, then add the apple juice. Completely seal the foil and return it to the smoker.

7. Continue to cook the shoulder for about 2 hours, until it reaches an internal temperature of 203°F.

8. Remove the pork from the smoker and allow it to rest for 30 minutes.

9. Using heat-resistant rubber gloves, transfer the shoulder to a deep aluminum tray. Pull the meat into 1- to 2-inch strips, discarding any extra bits of fat and the bone.

10. Add some of the remaining liquid from the foil, as needed, and sprinkle on more of the rub to taste.

Ingredient Tip: To add more heat and twang, use hot sauce rather than mustard in step 3. Feel free to add some more into the foil packet when you wrap it to further infuse the flavor.

DRY BABY BACK RIBS

SERVES 6
PREP TIME: 20 MINUTES
REST TIME: 12 HOURS
COOK TIME: 5 HOURS

 SUGGESTED WOOD: **Hickory**

Nothing says Memphis-style barbecue more than dry-rubbed ribs. The rub combines the aromatic flavors of oregano, thyme, and cumin, while the apple cider vinegar spritz adds a tangy and fruity flavor and also contributes to a beautiful bark. These ribs are simple and no-nonsense, giving you time to sit back and enjoy the cook with friends and family.

3 racks baby back ribs

¾ cup Memphis
Barbecue Rub (page 84)

½ cup unfiltered
apple juice

½ cup apple
cider vinegar

1. Remove the membrane from the back of your ribs using a paper towel and trim any thick pieces of fat. Season the ribs generously with the rub, cover them in foil, and allow them to rest in the refrigerator for up to 12 hours.

2. Heat the smoker to 250°F with 3 chunks of wood.

3. Place the ribs in the smoker and cook for 1 hour.

4. Combine the apple juice and vinegar in a spray bottle. Spray each rib 3 times with a fine mist every 30 minutes. Do this step quickly to minimize heat loss.

5. The meat will begin to pull away from the bones about ¼ inch and will develop a deep mahogany color after 4½ to 5 hours. The ribs should bend easily when grasped by tongs, but the meat should not fall away from the bones. Check the doneness with an instant-read thermometer. The ideal temperature is around 195°F, which allows the collagens and fats to melt, making the meat tender and juicy.

6. Remove the ribs from the smoker and allow them to rest for 15 minutes on a cutting board. Season the ribs lightly with more of the rub before slicing and serving.

Pro Advice: If you have any leftover ribs, strip the meat off the bones and save it to use in your next batch of barbecue beans or chili. The meat flavor will take these dishes to a whole new level.

WET BABY BACK RIBS

SERVES 6
PREP TIME: 20 MINUTES
REST TIME: 12 HOURS
COOK TIME: 5 HOURS 30 MINUTES

 SUGGESTED WOOD: **Hickory**

One of the oldest culinary debates in the barbecue world: wet or dry? Some feel that you haven't eaten ribs if you don't need a handful of wet wipes to clean off all the sauce after you've licked your fingers. I say try both and decide for yourself which is your favorite.

3 racks baby back ribs

¾ cup Memphis
Barbecue Rub (page 84)

½ cup apple juice

½ cup apple
cider vinegar

1 cup Memphis Barbecue
Sauce (page 85)

1. Remove the membrane from the back of the ribs using a paper towel and trim any thick pieces of fat. Season the ribs generously with the rub, cover them in foil, and allow them to rest in the refrigerator for up to 12 hours.

2. Heat the smoker to 250°F with 3 chunks of wood.

3. Place the ribs in the smoker and cook for 1 hour.

4. Combine the apple juice and vinegar in a spray bottle. Spray each rib 3 times with a fine mist every 30 minutes. Do this step quickly to minimize heat loss.

5. The meat will begin to pull away from the bones about ¼ inch and will develop a deep mahogany color after about 4 hours.

6. Brush a liberal amount of sauce on the ribs and continue to cook. After 30 minutes, brush another coat of sauce on the ribs.

7. With your tongs, the ribs should bend easily but not fall away from the bones. Check the doneness with an instant-read thermometer. The ideal temperature is around 195°F, which allows the collagens and fats to melt, making the meat tender and juicy.

8. Remove the ribs from the smoker, apply another coat of sauce on the ribs, and allow them to rest for 15 minutes on a cutting board. Season the ribs lightly with more of the rub before slicing and serving.

Ingredient Tip: For a more apple-forward flavor on the ribs, substitute apple cider for the apple juice.

BARBECUE CORNISH HEN

SERVES 2

PREP TIME: 15 MINUTES

COOK TIME: 1 HOUR 30 MINUTES

 SUGGESTED WOOD: **Hickory**

Cornish game hens have a loyal cult following in the Memphis 'cue scene. The birds are smoked slowly, grilled over high heat using hickory or lump charcoal, and then finished off with plenty of sauce. When shopping, plan on one hen per person.

3 tablespoons sweet paprika

2 tablespoons dark brown sugar

2 tablespoons granulated sugar

2 tablespoons kosher salt

1 tablespoon freshly ground black pepper

1 teaspoon granulated garlic

1 teaspoon granulated onion

1 teaspoon mustard powder

½ teaspoon cayenne pepper

2 Cornish hens

1 cup of Memphis Barbecue Sauce (page 85)

Hot sauce (optional)

1. Preheat your smoker to 200°F with 2 chunks of wood.

2. In a small bowl, mix the paprika, brown sugar, granulated sugar, salt, black pepper, granulated garlic, granulated onion, mustard powder, and cayenne pepper together, and set aside.

3. Spatchcock the hens (see page 18).

4. Remove and discard the wing tips from the hens, and liberally season both sides of the birds with the rub.

5. Smoke the hens, meat-side down, for 1 hour. Remove the hens from the smoker and increase the temperature to 350°F.

6. Return the hens to the smoker, meat-side up.

7. While the meat is cooking, in a small saucepan over low heat, combine and warm the barbecue sauce and hot sauce (if using).

8. Cook the hens for 30 minutes more, until they reach an internal temperature of 160°F in the breast and 180° in the thigh.

9. Remove the hens from the smoker and allow them to rest for 10 minutes. Coat liberally in the barbecue sauce and serve.

Experiment: This recipe calls for hickory wood, which is traditional to the region, but Cozy Corner, the shop that made this recipe famous, only uses hard lump charcoal. If your cooker is made to handle lump charcoal, try cooking with it to see how it affects the flavor.

SMOKED BOLOGNA CHUB

SERVES 10 TO 12
PREP TIME: 20 MINUTES
COOK TIME: 4 HOURS

SUGGESTED WOOD: **Hickory or Pecan**

Forget about the processed bologna of your childhood. This flavorful, smoked variation will become your new favorite sandwich meat. Serve it sliced on potato buns with slaw, or dice it into cubes and serve it as an appetizer. You will never want to eat bologna again unless it is smoked.

3 tablespoons sweet paprika

2 tablespoons dark brown sugar

1 tablespoon freshly ground black pepper

2 teaspoons granulated garlic

2 teaspoons granulated onion

1 teaspoon celery seed

1 teaspoon mustard powder

1 (3- to 5-pound) bologna chub

3 tablespoons yellow mustard

½ cup Memphis Barbecue Sauce (page 85)

Potato rolls, for serving

Coleslaw, for serving

1. Preheat your smoker to 225°F with 2 chunks of wood.

2. In a small bowl, thoroughly mix the paprika, brown sugar, pepper, granulated garlic, granulated onion, celery seed, and mustard powder together, and set aside.

3. Using the tip of a sharp knife, score the surface of the bologna, lengthwise, about ⅛ inch deep. Repeat the process about every inch around the chub, for a total of eight lines from tip to stern.

4. Slather the bologna in the yellow mustard. The mustard acts as a binder for the seasoning and will impart very little flavor.

5. Generously season the bologna with the rub.

6. Place the bologna in the smoker and cook for 3 hours. Brush the outside of the bologna with the barbecue sauce and cook for 1 hour more, until the sauce is caramelized.

7. Remove the bologna from the smoker and cut it into ½-inch-thick slices. Serve sliced on potato rolls and topped with coleslaw.

Experiment: To make bologna burnt ends, when you remove the bologna from the smoker, cut it into one-inch cubes, apply another coat of barbecue sauce and rub, and return it to the smoker in an aluminum pan for 1 hour more.

Seven

Kentucky

The Story

There are 79 counties in Kentucky, and almost every one of them has its own style of barbecue. Though Kentucky is famous for its barbecue mutton, the true king of smoked meat here is pork, especially pork shoulder. In Western Kentucky, pulled or chopped pork reigns supreme, but a regional challenger is mutton served with a rich Worcestershire dip. In the south, they're famous for pork steaks cut from the shoulder and cooked over hickory coals, then smothered in a unique sauce made with butter, lard, and vinegar. In both the eastern and northern parts of the state, the influences of North Carolina and Tennessee appear, especially in their tomato- and vinegar-based sauces.

Best-Kept Secrets

» Kentucky is famous for barbecue mutton: meat from an older sheep that tends to have more fat and a gamey taste. But outside of the region, it may be difficult to find. However, you can always substitute lamb. When shopping for lamb, look for imported lamb rather than domestic. They tend to be grass fed rather than grain fed, which will be closer to mutton in taste.

» Worcestershire sauce is critical to Kentucky barbecue and can be found in nearly every dish throughout the state. Be sure to have copious amounts on hand.

» Hickory is, by far, the most prevalent wood for barbecue in the state. Depending on your smoker, be sure to use 100 percent pecan wood (a type of hickory), especially if you're using a pellet smoker, in order to get the full flavor of the smoke. If you're using lump charcoal, use one that is made from 100 percent pecan wood.

Classic Sides

Green beans are a popular side dish in Kentucky, and they're made in a variety of ways. Typically, the beans are stewed with fatty pork or ham and cooked until tender and rich. Some variants have them prepared in the smoker, absorbing the smoke and the flavorful steam from the cooking meats.

A good, heaping side of mac 'n' cheese makes the average Kentuckian swoon. Though many variations exist, you can expect extra amounts of cheese and butter, and, if you are really lucky, bits of bacon or ham.

Barbecue baked potatoes are also a standard side. You can find both white and sweet potatoes on menus throughout the state. They're cooked over a bed of hickory coals at a low temperature, allowing them to take on a smoky flavor and deliver a velvety texture.

KENTUCKY BARBECUE RUB

MAKES 1 CUP

PREP TIME: 5 MINUTES

This multipurpose barbecue rub pairs well with many of the pork and chicken dishes enjoyed throughout Central and Eastern Kentucky. This recipe features equal parts sweet paprika and chili powder for just the right mix of sweet and heat.

¼ cup sweet paprika

¼ cup chili powder

2 tablespoons dark brown sugar

2 tablespoons freshly ground black pepper

2 tablespoons kosher salt

2 tablespoons mustard powder

1 tablespoon granulated garlic

1 tablespoon granulated onion

2 teaspoons ground coriander

1 teaspoon cayenne pepper (optional)

1. In a medium bowl, combine all of the ingredients and mix thoroughly.

2. Store the rub in a cool, dark place in a sealable plastic or glass container for no more than 3 months. Spices will oxidize over time and will lose their flavor if stored for too long.

Ingredient Tip: This rub gets its heat from the chili powder, which can vary widely by brand. If you find that the heat level is too low, add the optional cayenne pepper to raise the spiciness.

KENTUCKY WORCESTERSHIRE DIP

MAKES 3 CUPS
PREP TIME: 15 MINUTES
COOK TIME: 30 MINUTES

Just about every barbecue joint or church festival in Western Kentucky serves this regional favorite dip, which is also known as Kentucky Black Sauce. It pairs well with fatty meats and can cut the gamey taste of mutton and lamb. Pour it over pulled lamb or pork, or use it as a dip for sandwiches.

2 cups water

½ cup Worcestershire sauce

¼ cup apple cider vinegar

⅓ cup dark brown sugar

2 tablespoons lemon juice

1 teaspoon freshly ground black pepper

½ teaspoon kosher salt

½ teaspoon garlic powder

½ teaspoon onion powder

½ teaspoon ground cinnamon

½ teaspoon ground cloves

¼ teaspoon nutmeg

½ teaspoon white pepper

1. In a medium saucepot over medium-high heat, combine all of the ingredients and bring them to a boil.

2. Reduce the heat and simmer for 30 minutes.

3. Remove the dip from the heat and serve with lamb or pork.

Pro Advice: This dip can also be used as a basting liquid. Use a brush or run the sauce through a fine-mesh strainer and pour it into a compression sprayer to baste your meat.

CIDER-BRINED PORK SHOULDER

SERVES 10 TO 12
PREP TIME: 1 HOUR
BRINE TIME: 4 TO 8 HOURS
COOK TIME: 10 TO 12 HOURS

 SUGGESTED WOOD: **Hickory**

Kentucky's take on pulled pork features an apple cider and vinegar brine that is injected deep into the meat and mopped during cooking. This method accentuates the flavor of the meat and hickory wood alike. For the best results, allow extra time in this recipe for the brine to work its magic overnight. This meat arrives so flavorful that no sauce will be required.

For the brine/mop

6 cups apple cider

3 cups apple cider vinegar

2 cups water

½ cup kosher salt

½ cup dark brown sugar

½ cup Worcestershire sauce

⅓ cup Kentucky Barbecue Rub (page 100)

1 tablespoon granulated garlic

1 tablespoon granulated onion

1. **To make the brine/mop:** In a medium saucepot over medium high heat, combine all of the brine ingredients and bring them to a boil, stirring until all the salt and sugar crystals have completely dissolved. Divide the brine into 2 equal amounts and set them aside to fully cool.

2. **To make the meat:** Using a heavy-duty meat injector, inject the liquid from one of the brine solutions into the meat roughly every inch. Inject the needle all the way into the meat and push in the plunger as you pull out the needle. When complete, tightly wrap the pork in plastic wrap and let it rest in the refrigerator at least 4 hours or up to 8 hours.

3. Preheat your smoker to 225°F with 4 chunks of wood.

4. Remove the pork from the refrigerator and liberally cover it in the rub.

5. Place the pork, fat-side up, in the smoker and baste it with the remaining brine every 30 minutes. Replenish the wood chunks as needed.

For the meat

1 (8- to 9-pound) pork shoulder

⅓ cup Kentucky Barbecue Rub (page 100)

6. Smoke for at least 8 hours, or until it reaches an internal temperature of 180°F.

7. Lay out a double-thick layer of foil and put the pork shoulder in the middle. Fold up the side of the foil and add ½ cup of the brine. Completely seal the foil and return it to the smoker.

8. Smoke for another 2 hours, or until the internal temperature reaches 200°F. Remove the pork from the smoker and allow it to rest in a cooler for 1 hour.

9. Remove the pork from the cooler and, using heat-resistant rubber gloves or forks, pull the pork into thin strips. Add any remaining brine to taste.

Pro Advice: I called for a mop of the brine in this recipe, but you can also use a compression sprayer. I suggest running the brine through a fine-mesh strainer to catch any large pieces of spice prior to pouring it into the sprayer to avoid a clogged nozzle.

MONROE COUNTY PULLED PORK SHOULDER

SERVES 12
PREP TIME: 15 MINUTES
COOK TIME: 10 TO 12 HOURS

 SUGGESTED WOOD: **Hickory**

Kentucky's South-Central region offers a distinctive and largely unknown barbecue style. This Monroe County favorite traditionally features slices of pork shoulder grilled quickly over hickory coals and served with a vinegar- and lard-based dip. This low and slow variation offers a little known example of regional American cooking that's likely to impress your crew.

4 cups distilled vinegar

½ cup lard

½ cup salted butter

4 tablespoons kosher salt, divided

3 tablespoons freshly ground black pepper, divided

2 tablespoons cayenne pepper

1 (8-pound) pork shoulder

1. In a saucepan over low heat, cook the vinegar, lard, butter, 3 tablespoons of the salt, 2 tablespoons of the pepper, and the cayenne until combined. Continue to keep the sauce warm to keep the fat melted.

2. Heat the smoker to 250°F and add 3 chunks of wood.

3. In a small bowl, combine the remaining 1 tablespoon of salt and 1 tablespoon of pepper, and season the pork liberally with the mixture.

4. Cook the pork in the smoker, fat cap–side up. After 4 hours, brush the pork with the dip every hour for 4 hours more.

5. Once the shoulder has reached an internal temperature of 170°F, wrap it in two layers of heavy-duty foil. Fold up the sides of the foil to create a bowl around the shoulder, pour ½ cup of the dip in with the pork, then completely seal the shoulder in the foil.

6. Return the pork to the smoker and cook another 4 hours, or until the internal temperature reaches 205°F. Remove the pork from the smoker and allow it to rest for 30 minutes.

7. Open the foil carefully and place the contents in a disposable aluminum pan. Using heat-resistant rubber gloves, pull the pork into strips, discarding any visible fat. Serve the pork with extra sauce for dipping.

Ingredient Tip: The ideal vinegar used in this dish is distilled colored vinegar, which is distilled white vinegar with caramel coloring added, and has a lower acidity level.

PICKLE-BRINED BARBECUE CHICKEN

SERVES 6
PREP TIME: 15 MINUTES
BRINE TIME: 6 TO 14 HOURS
COOK TIME: 2 HOURS 30 MINUTES

 SUGGESTED WOOD: **Hickory**

The next time you go to recycle that empty pickle jar, don't throw away the juice. It can be used to make this incredibly moist Memphis chicken recipe. I love to pair the meat with a homemade honey mustard sauce and a touch of hot sauce. The pickle brine adds a vinegar flavor without overpowering the meat.

For the chicken

2 whole (3- to 3½-pound) fryer chickens

2 cups dill pickle juice

2 cups buttermilk

½ cup Kentucky Barbecue Rub (see page 100)

For the sauce

½ cup mayonnaise

2 tablespoons Dijon mustard

2 tablespoons honey

1 tablespoon yellow mustard

1½ teaspoons lemon juice

1 teaspoon vinegar-based hot sauce

1. **To make the chicken:** Spatchcock the chickens (see page 18).

2. Place each chicken in its own gallon zip-top bag, along with 1 cup each of the pickle juice. Remove all the air from the bags and seal them tightly. Place the bags in the refrigerator, meat-side down, for at least 4 hours and as long as 12 hours. Flip the meat over occasionally to make sure all parts of the chicken get the brine.

3. Remove the chicken from the refrigerator and pour out the pickle juice. Add 1 cup of buttermilk to each bag and return them to the refrigerator for 2 hours, meat-side down.

4. Preheat your smoker to 250°F with 2 chunks of wood.

5. Remove the chickens from the refrigerator and place them on a baking sheet, discarding the buttermilk. Liberally season the chicken all over with the rub.

6. Place the chickens in the smoker, meat-side up, and cook for 2 ½ hours, or until the internal temperature at the thickest part of the breast reads 165°F.

7. Remove the chickens from the smoker and allow them to rest for 20 minutes.

8. **To make the sauce:** While the chickens are resting, whisk all of the sauce ingredients together and set aside.

9. Slice the chickens and serve with the honey mustard sauce.

Experiment: I used dill pickle juice for this recipe, but feel free to be creative with spicier ones.

BARBECUE MUTTON WITH WORCESTERSHIRE DIP

SERVES 8 TO 10

PREP TIME: 15 MINUTES

COOK TIME: 5 TO 6 HOURS

 SUGGESTED WOOD: **Hickory**

Often, you hear stories of how a particular style of barbecue originated with an abundance of a particular meat that was too tough or gamey to cook unless smoked low and slow. Such is the case with barbecue mutton in Kentucky, where a Worcestershire-based mop is used to cut through the meat's gaminess, while the slow cooking method breaks down the protein.

For the mop sauce

1⅔ cups water

1 cup apple cider vinegar

⅔ cup Worcestershire sauce

¼ cup kosher salt

2 tablespoons freshly squeezed lemon juice

1 teaspoon freshly ground black pepper

1. **To make the mop sauce:** In a medium saucepot over medium-high heat, combine all of the mop ingredients and bring them to a boil. Reduce the heat to the lowest setting.

2. **To make the meat:** Preheat your smoker to 250°F with 2 chunks of wood.

3. Slather the mutton in the yellow mustard and generously season the meat with the salt and pepper.

4. Place the mutton in the smoker and cook for 5 to 6 hours, basting the meat with the mop sauce every 30 minutes and replenishing the wood chunks as needed, until the internal temperature at the thickest part of the meat reaches 195°F.

5. Remove the mutton from the smoker, double wrap it in foil, and allow it to rest in a cooler for 1 hour.

6. Heat the Worcestershire dip in a small saucepan over low heat until it comes to a simmer.

For the meat

1 (5- to 6-pound) mutton leg or shoulder

⅓ cup yellow mustard

2 tablespoons kosher salt

2 tablespoons freshly ground black pepper

2 cups Kentucky Worcestershire Dip (page 101)

Hamburger buns or white bread, for serving

7. Once the mutton has rested, remove the bone and pull the meat into thumb-size chunks. Add some of the Worcestershire dip and stir until fully incorporated into the meat.

8. Serve the pulled mutton with the remaining sauce for maximum moisture. Serve by itself or on toasted hamburger buns or white bread.

Ingredient Tip: If you're using lamb instead of mutton, be sure to keep an eye on your temperature. Lamb often cooks faster than mutton.

SMOKED CITY HAM

SERVES 8 TO 10
PREP TIME: 15 MINUTES
COOK TIME: 2 HOURS 30 MINUTES

 SUGGESTED WOOD: **Hickory**

A favorite on menus all over Western Kentucky, City Ham is a precooked ham that is reseasoned and smoked to impart a deeper smoke flavor. Try to find a minimally processed ham shank (the label should read "ham with water'" or "ham in natural juice").

1 (7- to 9-pound) ham shank

½ cup brown sugar

½ cup honey

¼ cup bourbon, preferably from Kentucky

2 tablespoons yellow mustard

½ teaspoon ground nutmeg

½ teaspoon ground allspice

1. Preheat your smoker to 225°F with 2 chunks of wood.

2. Rinse the ham in cold water and wipe it dry with a paper towel.

3. Score the outside of the ham with a sharp knife in a diamond pattern, or a pattern of your choosing.

4. Place the ham in the smoker and cook for about 2 hours, or until it reaches an internal temperature of 130°F.

5. In a medium saucepan over medium-low heat, combine the brown sugar, honey, bourbon, mustard, nutmeg, and allspice, whisking occasionally, until fully incorporated. Remove the glaze from the heat.

6. Brush the glaze on the ham every 15 minutes, until the ham reaches an internal temperature of 145°F in the thickest part of the meat.

7. Remove the ham from the smoker, loosely cover it with foil, and allow it to rest for 15 minutes prior to slicing and serving.

Ingredient Tip: You can substitute the yellow mustard with Dijon mustard in the glaze for a spicier flavor.

Eight

North Carolina

The Story

North Carolina has many barbecue subregions with their own flavor profiles, and each region will defend their 'cue as the definitive champion. But why not try them all? This chapter kicks off with two of the main regional creations—Eastern North Carolina barbecue, which uses a vinegar-based sauce (and never any tomato), and Lexington-area 'cue, which specializes in tangy dip that includes ketchup or tomato sauce.

Best-Kept Secrets

» For the most authentic barbecue, you will want to use wood that is common to the area. In North Carolina, hickory is the most prevalent choice for barbecue wood, but white oak is common, as well. Both of these have different flavor profiles, and I suggest mixing and matching these woods to find a ratio that produces the flavor you like best.

» In North Carolina, the traditional method of cooking is low and slow over open pit barbecues, which in most residential areas, is difficult to do. For this region, if you have a bullet or kamado smoker, remove the water pan or heat grate to allow the fat and meat juices to drop down onto the coals.

» One secret ingredient I share in this chapter is the use of Vietnamese fish sauce, an ingredient that's fairly new to the North Carolina barbecue scene. A small amount of this sauce will add a savory, umami flavor to your meat. However, a little bit of fish sauce goes a long way, so slowly add it to your sauces or marinades to avoid overpowering them.

Classic Sides

Much like the sauces in North Carolina, there is a debate about which coleslaw is the best. The Dutch- and German-inspired slaw, sometimes referred to as "seven day slaw," has no mayonnaise, making it more shelf stable. The other primary coleslaw in the state is Piedmont-style slaw (also known as red slaw), which includes ketchup. Variations of this slaw will contain pimentos and bell peppers.

Finally, North Carolinians love anything coated with a fried cornmeal batter, such as hushpuppies or corn sticks. In the South, corn has been a staple grain since the Depression. Some variations are a little sour, thanks to buttermilk, while others use water or whole milk in the batter. You can even find hushpuppies dusted with powdered sugar and served as a dessert.

NC BARBECUE RUB

MAKES 2 CUPS

PREP TIME: 5 MINUTES

This versatile, bright red barbecue rub features sweet paprika and cayenne pepper balanced by the sweetness of light brown sugar. The addition of celery seed brings both savory and bitter notes, while the mustard powder adds some tang, making the rub appropriate for various meats.

½ cup sweet paprika

½ cup light brown sugar

¼ cup kosher salt

2 tablespoons chili powder

2 teaspoons cayenne pepper

2 teaspoons celery seed

2 teaspoons freshly ground black pepper

2 teaspoons granulated garlic

2 teaspoons granulated onion

2 teaspoons mustard powder

1. In a medium bowl, combine all of the ingredients and mix thoroughly.

2. Store the rub in a cool, dark place in a sealable plastic or glass container for no more than 3 months. Spices will oxidize over time and lose their flavor.

EASTERN NC BARBECUE SAUCE

SERVES 4 CUPS
PREP TIME: 5 MINUTES

Considered by many to be the mother of all American barbecue sauces, this sauce's origins trace back more than 200 years in North Carolina. Unlike many other barbecue sauces, this one uses no ketchup and relies on the tangy flavor of apple cider vinegar and the spice of the pepper flakes. It can be used as a dip, a marinade, and even a basting mop during cooking.

4 cups apple cider vinegar

3 tablespoons freshly ground black pepper

3 tablespoons dark brown sugar

2 tablespoons red pepper flakes

4 teaspoons kosher salt

1½ tablespoons vinegar-based hot sauce

In a sealable container, such as a mason jar, mix all of the ingredients thoroughly until the salt and sugar dissolve.

Pro Advice: As there are no perishable ingredients in this sauce, it can be stored for up to a year. But given that spices will oxidize and lose their flavor over time, I recommend that you use it within three months.

Experiment: If you really want to step up the umami flavor of this sauce, add a tablespoon of Vietnamese fish sauce. Typically made from fermented anchovies and salt, it will add an incredibly savory flavor to pork dishes.

LEXINGTON DIP SAUCE

MAKES 5 CUPS
PREP TIME: 5 MINUTES
COOK TIME: 10 MINUTES
REST TIME: 4 TO 24 HOURS

On the other side of the North Carolina sauce debate is this Lexington recipe, which is similar to its Eastern cousin but adds the tangy flavor of ketchup, which was introduced to the region in the late 1800s.

3 cups apple cider vinegar

1 cup water

1 cup ketchup

2 tablespoons dark brown sugar

1 tablespoon vinegar-based hot sauce

2 teaspoons freshly ground black pepper

2 teaspoons red pepper flakes

2 teaspoons kosher salt

1. In a medium saucepot over medium heat, combine all of the ingredients and bring them to a simmer, stirring until all the salt and sugar crystals have completely dissolved. Set aside to cool.

2. Transfer the sauce into a sealable jar and refrigerate it for at least 4 hours, but ideally up to 24 hours.

Pro Advice: This sauce can be used as a finishing dip for your meat or as a glaze on ribs. During the final hour of cooking, lightly brush it over ribs every 20 minutes to achieve an admirable glaze—sticky, but not overly wet.

EASTERN NC RIBS

SERVES 6
PREP TIME: 20 MINUTES
REST TIME: 12 HOURS
COOK TIME: 5 HOURS

 SUGGESTED WOOD: **Oak or Hickory**

North Carolina barbecue is usually pork served pulled, shredded, or chopped, but this recipe celebrates the baby back rib. These ribs are leaner than spareribs and are perfectly accentuated by the combined flavors of a rub and a vinegar-based sauce. Watch the smoker's temperature on these, as baby back ribs cook faster than spareribs.

3 racks baby back ribs

¾ cup NC Barbecue Rub (page 116)

4 cups Eastern NC Barbecue Sauce (page 117), divided

1. Remove the membrane from the back of the ribs using a paper towel and trim any thick pieces of fat. Season the ribs generously with the rub, cover them in foil, and allow them to rest in the refrigerator for up to 12 hours.

2. Heat the smoker to 250°F with 3 chunks of wood.

3. Place the ribs in the smoker and cook for about 5 hours, basting the meat with the mop sauce every 30 minutes. Replenish the wood chunks as needed.

4. Using tongs, test the ribs for doneness. The ribs should bend easily but not fall away from the meat, which should be a deep mahogany color. Once the ribs reach 195°F, remove them from the smoker, apply another coat of sauce, and place them on a cutting board. Lightly cover them with foil and allow them to rest for 15 minutes.

5. Season the ribs lightly with any remaining rub before slicing. Serve with the remaining sauce as a dip for the ribs.

EASTERN NC PULLED PORK

SERVES 10
PREP TIME: 15 MINUTES
COOK TIME: 10 TO 12 HOURS

 SUGGESTED WOOD: **Oak or Hickory**

By using oak wood when smoking this butt, along with a tangy, vinegar-based sauce, your pork will be bursting with flavor. I find that too much fat is trimmed away in most mass-market pork, allowing the meat to dry out, which is why I recommend wrapping the pork in foil.

2 cups apple
cider vinegar

½ cup water

¼ cup vegetable oil

¼ cup lightly packed
brown sugar

3 tablespoons red
pepper flakes

1 tablespoon kosher salt

2 teaspoons freshly
ground black pepper

1 tablespoon hot sauce

1 (8-pound) pork
shoulder or Boston butt

1. In a medium bowl, combine the vinegar, water, oil, brown sugar, red pepper flakes, salt, black pepper, and hot sauce, and whisk to combine.

2. Heat the smoker to 250°F with 2 chunks of wood (unless you're not using an offset cooker; see tip).

3. Place the pork, fat-side up, in your smoker for about 8 hours, adding 2 chunks of wood every hour), or until it reaches an internal temperate of 170°F.

4. Lay out a double-thick layer of foil and place the pork in the middle. Fold up the sides of the foil to create a bowl, then add ½ cup of the prepared sauce. Wrap and completely seal the pork and sauce in the foil and return it to the smoker.

5. Cook for 4 hours more, or until the internal temperature reaches 200°F.

6. Remove the pork from the smoker. Do not remove it from the foil. Instead, wrap the foil-covered meat in a towel and place it in a cooler for at least 30 minutes to rest.

7. Wearing heat-resistant rubber gloves, tear the pork into thin strips, discarding any visible fat.

8. Toss the meat with the sauce in small amounts at a time, adding more to taste.

Pro Advice: If you're not using an offset smoker, you can save time by placing two wood chunks in a disposable pan and another two chunks in a separate disposable pan partially filled with water. About the time the first two chunks are finished, the water will have evaporated, and the wood will begin to smoke. Alternate the process until step 4.

LEXINGTON NAKED CHOPPED PORK

SERVES 10
PREP TIME: 15 MINUTES
COOK TIME: 8 HOURS

 SUGGESTED WOOD: **Hickory**

This recipe is a pure celebration of pork. It's cooked "naked" with only some kosher salt, and then finished off with tangy Lexington Dip Sauce. The salt is added after an hour in the smoker so that the meat builds up its own moisture for the salt to adhere to. In true Lexington style, this pork is coarsely chopped and never pulled.

1 (9- to 10-pound) pork shoulder or Boston butt

3 tablespoons kosher salt

2 cups Lexington Dip Sauce (page 118)

White hamburger buns, for serving

1. Preheat your smoker to 275°F with 4 chunks of wood.

2. Using a sharp knife, trim off any excess fat and blood spots you may see on the shoulder.

3. Place the pork in the smoker, fat-side down, and cook for 1 hour, until a coating of moisture resembling sweat appears on the pork.

4. Using large tongs to roll the pork over, liberally apply the salt to the shoulder. Continue to cook, fat-side down, for 7 hours more, or until the internal temperature at the thickest part reaches 195°F. Replenish the wood chunks as required.

5. Remove the pork from the smoker, double wrap it in foil, and place it in a cooler to rest for 1 hour.

6. Remove the shoulder from the cooler and place it in a deep aluminum pan. Remove and discard the bone and any unrendered fat and tear the pork into 1- to 2-inch strips.

7. Using a cleaver or large chef's knife, coarsely chop the pork. Pour 1 cup of the dip sauce over the chopped pork, and then thoroughly mix the meat and sauce together, adding more sauce as needed. Serve on white hamburger buns.

Pro Advice: A modern hard-cased cooler can keep the pork hot for four to five hours if you need to prepare it ahead of time. To prep your cooler, pour three gallons of hot tap water into it and seal the lid for 30 minutes. Then, pour out the hot water and place a towel on the bottom of the cooler. Place the foil-wrapped pork on the towel, and then cover it with a second towel. Be sure to check your meat, ensuring that it has not dropped below 140°F before serving.

LEXINGTON SMOKED PORK PICNIC

SERVES 12
PREP TIME: 15 MINUTES
COOK TIME: 8 TO 9 HOURS

 SUGGESTED WOOD: **Hickory or Oak**

This recipe uses the pork's "picnic" cut, which be found adjacent to the butt just before the shank. It's a fattier cut, and its large bone provides mouthwatering flavor. A spritz of apple juice, pineapple juice, and vinegar will keep the meat moist and help adhere the smoke to the meat.

1 (10- to 11-pound) picnic cut pork

3 tablespoons sorghum molasses or regular molasses

½ cup NC Barbecue Rub (page 116)

1 cup apple juice

1 cup pineapple juice

1 cup apple cider vinegar

3 cups Lexington Dip Sauce (page 118)

1. Preheat your smoker to 250°F with 4 chunks of wood.

2. Using a sharp knife, trim any excess fat or skin from the pork.

3. Rub the pork down with the molasses. Liberally season the pork with the barbecue rub.

4. Mix the apple juice, pineapple juice, and vinegar together in a compression sprayer and prime.

5. Place the pork in the smoker and cook for 5 hours, lightly spraying the meat with the juice and replenishing the wood chunks every 1 hour.

6. Remove the pork from the smoker, spritz one last time, and double wrap it in foil. Return the pork to the smoker and cook for 3 to 4 hours more, or until the internal temperature reaches 200°F.

7. Remove the pork from the smoker and carefully open the foil. Brush the pork with the dip sauce and return it to the smoker for 15 to 20 minutes, until the sauce thickens up like a glaze.

8. Remove the pork from the smoker and allow it to rest for 20 minutes. Pull apart the pork, removing any unrendered pieces of fat, then coarsely chop the meat. Add more dip sauce to taste, toss together, and serve.

Ingredient Tip: Sorghum molasses is prevalent in North Carolina, but it may be difficult to find outside of the South. If you can't find sorghum molasses, you can substitute regular sugarcane molasses, honey, or even agave.

ORANGE-CRUSTED PORK RIB ROAST

SERVES 8 TO 10
PREP TIME: 15 MINUTES
COOK TIME: 3 HOURS

 SUGGESTED WOOD: **Hickory**

If you are looking to keep the North Carolina theme on the menu for a holiday or special occasion, try making this pork rib roast. This recipe uses a wet rub instead of a traditional dry rub, helping seal in the moisture. The smell of roasting orange marmalade and rosemary easily conjures holiday spirits.

½ cup Dijon mustard

3 tablespoons orange marmalade

2 tablespoons kosher salt

2 tablespoons orange juice

2 tablespoons Worcestershire sauce

1½ tablespoons freshly ground black pepper

1 tablespoon freshly chopped rosemary

3 to 4 freshly minced garlic cloves

1 (5- to 6-pound) bone-in pork rib roast

1. Heat the smoker to 275°F with 3 chunks of wood.

2. Whisk the mustard, marmalade, salt, orange juice, Worcestershire sauce, pepper, rosemary, and garlic together in a small bowl and set aside.

3. Brush the wet rub over the entire rib roast.

4. Place the roast in the smoker, rib-side down, and cook for 3 hours, or until it reaches an internal temperature of 145°F.

5. Remove the roast from the smoker and allow it to rest for 15 minutes before slicing.

Experiment: If you are looking to add a bit more flavor, after you brush on the wet rub, sprinkle the meat with three tablespoons of NC Barbecue Rub (page 116). Not only will you get the great flavors of this rub, but you will also have a great orange color from the smoked paprika.

SMOKED SUCKLING PIG

SERVES 12
PREP TIME: 15 MINUTES
COOK TIME: 7 HOURS

SUGGESTED WOOD: **Oak and Hickory**

 Cooking a whole pig is the apex of backyard barbecue, and it is an experience you and your guests will never forget. Before you dive straight into smoking a suckling pig, measure out the cooking surface of your smoker and find a pig that gives at least three to four inches of airflow all around your pig to ensure even cooking.

½ cup NC Barbecue Rub (page 116)

¼ cup kosher salt

2 tablespoons freshly ground black pepper

32 ounces apple cider

1 cup apple cider vinegar

1 (20- to 30-pound) suckling pig

½ cup vegetable oil

1. Heat the smoker to 225°F with 2 chunks of oak and 2 chunks of hickory wood.

2. In a small bowl, mix together the barbecue rub, salt, and pepper, and set aside.

3. In another small bowl, mix together the apple cider and vinegar, and set aside.

4. Place the suckling pig on a large cutting board, skin-side down. Using a sharp knife, cut through the breastbone, allowing the chest cavity to open freely. Press down gently on the sides of the pig until it lies flat.

5. Trim away any excess fat and blood-colored areas from the cavity.

6. Using a meat injector, inject the apple cider mixture into the meat, being sure to get extra into the shoulder and loin areas of the pig. Wipe down the cavity with paper towels.

7. Season the cavity thoroughly with the spice rub. Place the pig on a large baking sheet, cavity-side down, and wipe the skin down with paper towel. Wrap the snout and ears in foil to prevent burning.

8. Put the pig in the smoker, placing the head farthest away from the heat source. Cook for 3 hours, and then lightly rub the skin down with the oil using a barbecue mop or basting brush.

9. Smoke for 4 hours more, or until the internal temperature reads 190°F to 195°F in the deepest part of the shoulder.

10. Remove the pig from the smoker and allow it to rest for 30 minutes before picking and serving.

Pro Advice: Serve this pig with either the Lexington Dip Sauce (page 118) or Eastern NC Barbecue Sauce (page 117).

WHOLE SMOKED PORK SHOULDER

SERVES 12
PREP TIME: 20 MINUTES
COOK TIME: 16 TO 18 HOURS

 SUGGESTED WOOD: **Hickory**

A whole pork shoulder typically weighs around 20 pounds and includes both the Boston butt and the lower portion called the picnic cut, providing you with a diverse range of flavors. The picnic cut has a high fat content and a large bone in the middle, both of which contribute to its flavor and moistness. This recipe takes a considerable amount of time to make, so be sure to plan ahead.

32 ounces apple cider

1 cup apple cider vinegar

3 tablespoons Vietnamese fish sauce

1 (18- to 20-pound) whole pork shoulder

3 tablespoons yellow mustard

½ cup NC Barbecue Rub (page 116), plus more for dusting

4 cups Lexington Dip Sauce (page 118), divided

1. Heat the smoker to 225°F with 4 chunks of wood.

2. In a medium bowl, mix together the apple cider, vinegar, and fish sauce, and set aside.

3. Using a sharp knife, trim any skin from the shoulder and any thick globs of fat, as those will not render down.

4. Slather the pork with the mustard, and then generously season the pork with the rub.

5. Using a meat injector, inject the apple cider mixture into the meat at 1 inch intervals. For the best results, poke the meat with the needle, and then inject the liquid as you withdraw the needle. Reserve the remaining liquid.

6. Place an aluminum pan with water close to the heat source in the smoker. This will provide moisture, which keeps the meat from drying out.

7. Place the shoulder in the smoker and cook for 12 hours, or until the internal temperature at the thickest part reaches 160°F. Continue checking the water level and wood chunks at least every 2 hours.

8. Double wrap the shoulder in foil, adding 1 cup of the apple juice injection liquid before sealing. Return the pork to the smoker and cook for 5 to 6 hours more, or until the internal temperature reaches 195°F.

9. Remove the pork from the smoker and allow it to rest for 30 minutes. Carefully open the foil and transfer the pork to a rimmed baking sheet, reserving the liquid in the foil.

10. Using heat-resistant rubber gloves, pull the pork apart into 2-inch chunks. Then, using a cleaver or large chef's knife, coarsely chop the pork. Add 2 cups of the dip sauce and reserved liquid from the foil as needed. Dust the meat with some of the rub. Serve with the remaining dip sauce.

Pro Advice: To create a syrupy glaze on the pork, use one cup of the Lexington Dip Sauce with ¼ cup of the apple cider injection liquid when you are wrapping it in foil in step 8. This will allow the sauce to incorporate into the meat further by combining with the juices that will collect in the foil.

BUTTER-DIPPED CHICKEN

SERVES 6 TO 8
PREP TIME: 20 MINUTES
COOK TIME: 3 HOURS

 SUGGESTED WOOD: **Hickory**

This old-school chicken recipe, hailing from the Lexington area, features a butter- and apple cider vinegar–based sauce. Keep the sauce warm on the stove top during the cooking process to keep the butter from solidifying.

2 cups apple
cider vinegar

2 cups water

½ cup salted butter

2 tablespoons freshly
squeezed lemon juice

1½ teaspoons freshly
ground black pepper

1 (3- to 4-pound)
fryer chicken

¼ cup NC Barbecue Rub
(page 116)

1. Preheat your smoker to 275°F with 2 chunks of wood.

2. In a medium saucepot over medium-high heat, combine the vinegar, water, butter, lemon juice, and pepper, and bring them to a boil. Reduce to a simmer over low heat.

3. Spatchcock the chicken (see page 18). Sprinkle the barbecue rub over both sides of the chicken.

4. Place the chicken in the smoker, meat-side down, and cook for 1 hour, basting it with the butter sauce every 20 minutes.

5. Flip the chicken over and baste it again with the butter sauce. Cook for 1½ hours more, basting the chicken with the butter sauce every 20 minutes, until the internal temperature reaches 165°F at the thickest part of the breast.

6. Remove the chicken from the smoker and allow it to rest on a rimmed baking sheet. Slice the chicken and baste it one last time with the butter sauce.

Pro Advice: Add a tablespoon of the NC Barbecue Rub to the butter sauce to complement the rub you sprinkled on the chicken.

Nine

South Carolina

135

The Story

South Carolina loves its pork. In fact, most residents would say any meat can be barbecued, but only pork is barbecue. The state has four main regions, each featuring its own sauce. Mustard sauce, also known as Carolina Gold, is found in the Midlands. The upper part of the state, meanwhile, favors a light tomato- and vinegar-based creation known as Pee Dee sauce. Along the coastal regions, you'll find one of the original barbecue sauces, a spicy vinegar and pepper sauce that dates back a few hundred years. Finally, in the Northwest, you'll find a heavy tomato sauce similar in taste to KC Barbecue Sauce (page 51). In this chapter, we've included recipes for the less common mustard and Pee Dee sauces.

Best Kept Secrets

» Don't mess with the mustard. The gold standard (pun intended) for mustard sauce is the classic American yellow variety. The tangy flavors of its mustard seeds and vinegar are critical to the flavor of this sauce. Though it was likely not the mustard used by the original immigrants to the region, it has become the go-to ingredient.

» Cayenne pepper is used in many South Carolina barbecue dishes. Be sure to add it slowly to your rubs and sauces to ensure that they don't come out too spicy.

Classic Side Dishes

A quintessential Southern dish cooked throughout the state, collard greens are slow cooked for hours in a pot along with a smoky ham hock or bacon ends. The best versions use apple cider vinegar, which pairs with the barbecued meats and sauces of the region. If you happen to visit one of these barbecue joints or make it yourself, be sure to drink up some of the remaining liquid from the bottom of the pot, known as pot likker, which features a ton of flavor and much of the vitamins from the greens.

There are literally hundreds of variations of Brunswick stew throughout the state, but the one thing they have in common is they're all just downright delicious. This kitchen-sink side dish typically features peas, corn, onions, garlic, potatoes, and leftover chipped barbecue. The meat choices are endless but usually include pork and chicken, though some variations are known to have brisket and turkey. This dish is slow cooked for hours in a pot until fully incorporated into a stew.

Green beans might not be something you think of when it comes to barbecue, but this dish can be found at just about any barbecue joint throughout the state. Typically cooked with pork fat and chunks of bacon, how can you go wrong? Some places go highbrow and use fresh green beans, whereas the norm is to use canned green beans.

SC BARBECUE RUB

MAKES 2 CUPS
PREP TIME: 5 MINUTES

This is a classic South Carolina rub. The flavors of the rub pair best with pork and poultry, but feel free to experiment with other proteins. The mustard base in this rub is a nod to the German settlers of South Carolina, who brought their mustard preferences to the region. Try this dry rub the next time you're smoking, grilling, or slow-roasting and looking for that South Carolina flavor. Use all the ingredients or customize it to your taste.

1 cup light brown sugar

2 tablespoons chili powder

2 tablespoons freshly ground pepper

2 tablespoons granulated garlic

2 tablespoons ground cumin

2 tablespoons granulated onion

2 tablespoons kosher salt

2 tablespoons smoked paprika

1 tablespoon cayenne pepper

1 tablespoon dry mustard

1 tablespoon white pepper (optional; see tip)

1. In a medium bowl, combine all of the ingredients and mix thoroughly.

2. Store the rub in a cool, dark place in a sealable plastic or glass container for no more than 3 months.

Ingredient Tip: For added flavor on large cuts of pork, add the optional white pepper to this rub. The white pepper imparts a stronger pepper flavor than just the black pepper, and large cuts like pork shoulder can handle it.

PEE DEE TOMATO BARBECUE SAUCE

MAKES 4 CUPS
PREP TIME: 5 MINUTES
COOK TIME: 40 MINUTES

The Pee Dee region sits in South Carolina's northeastern corner, and is so named for the Pee Dee River and the Native American tribe that shares its name. This tomato-based barbecue sauce is lighter and less syrupy than the sauces popular elsewhere in South Carolina that rely more intently on ketchup and tomatoes.

3 cups apple
cider vinegar

½ cup ketchup

¼ cup red pepper flakes

¼ cup freshly ground
black pepper

2 tablespoons dark
brown sugar

½ teaspoon kosher salt

1. In a medium saucepot over medium-high heat, combine all of the ingredients, stirring until the sauce reaches a boil.

2. Reduce the heat to low and simmer for 30 minutes.

3. If stored in a tightly sealed container in the refrigerator, this sauce will keep for up to 1 month.

CAROLINA GOLD BARBECUE SAUCE

MAKES 2 CUPS
PREP TIME: 10 MINUTES
REST TIME: 24 HOURS

South Carolinians can all agree that low and slow barbecue is deeply rooted in their state's heritage, but when it comes to barbecue sauce, they are totally divided over the four regional variations. Many a backyard barbecue has ended in a "best sauce" debate. This mustard-based sauce, exclusive to South Carolina, could arguably be considered the state's unofficial barbecue sauce.

1½ cups yellow mustard

½ cup apple
cider vinegar

6 tablespoons dark
brown sugar

2 tablespoons ketchup

2 teaspoons
Worcestershire sauce

2 teaspoons
vinegar-based hot sauce

1 teaspoon freshly
ground black pepper

1 teaspoon kosher salt

½ teaspoon
granulated garlic

½ teaspoon
granulated onion

1. Place all of the ingredients in a pint-size mason jar and seal the lid.

2. Shake the jar for about 5 minutes until fully incorporated.

3. Place the jar in the refrigerator for at least 24 hours to allow the flavors to develop.

4. Allow the sauce to come to room temperature and shake before serving.

Pro Advice: If you are in hurry and forgot to make this sauce a day in advance, whisk together all of the ingredients in a non-reactive pot and simmer it on low for about 20 minutes, until the sugar has fully incorporated.

CHARLESTON SPARERIBS

SERVES 6
PREP TIME: 15 MINUTES
COOK TIME: 4 HOURS 30 MINUTES

 SUGGESTED WOOD: **Hickory and Oak**

A true pork lover's dream, these spareribs are smoked with oak and hickory. There is no sauce for this recipe, which is designed to celebrate the meaty flavor of the spareribs with just the right note of smokiness. For those who are minimalists and want the meat to shine, this recipe is for you.

2 tablespoons kosher salt

2 tablespoons sweet paprika

2 tablespoons chili powder

2 tablespoons light brown sugar

2 tablespoons granulated garlic

2 tablespoons granulated onion

1 tablespoon Ac'cent flavor enhancer

1 tablespoon cayenne pepper

1 tablespoon freshly ground black pepper

3 slabs pork spareribs

1. Preheat your smoker to 225°F with 2 chunks of hickory and 2 chunks of oak.

2. In a small bowl, mix the salt, paprika, chili powder, brown sugar, granulated garlic, granulated onion, Ac'cent, cayenne pepper, and black pepper together, and set aside.

3. Trim any fat from the ribs and remove the membrane from the bone side of each slab. Moderately season both sides of the ribs with the rub mix.

4. Place the spareribs in the smoker and cook for about 4½ hours, until the internal temperature reaches 195°F and the meat begins to pull away from the bone. Holding one end of the ribs with a pair of tongs, the ribs should bend in the middle but not break.

5. Remove the ribs from the smoker and allow them to rest 15 minutes before serving.

Ingredient Tip: Feel free to substitute the Ac'cent with a half tablespoon of chicken bouillon.

SC PULLED CHICKEN

SERVES 8
PREP TIME: 5 MINUTES
COOK TIME: 2 HOURS 15 MINUTES

 SUGGESTED WOOD: **Hickory**

At the risk of being accused of blasphemy, you've got to switch up the protein in your barbecue. This recipe uses chicken thighs for their high fat content and juiciness.

12 chicken thighs, bone in, skin on

⅓ cup SC Barbecue Rub (page 138)

1 cup Pee Dee Tomato Barbecue Sauce (page 139)

Hamburger buns, for serving

1. Preheat your smoker to 250°F with 2 chunks of wood.

2. Liberally season the chicken thighs with the barbecue rub. Place the chicken in the smoker, skin-side down, and cook for 1 hour.

3. Flip the chicken over and smoke for 30 minutes more, or until the meat reaches an internal temperature of 145°F.

4. Remove the chicken from the smoker and wrap it tightly in foil, making sure to seal up all the edges.

5. Return the chicken to the smoker and cook for 45 minutes more, or until the internal temperature reaches 175°F. Remove the chicken from the smoker and allow it to rest for 10 minutes.

6. Open the foil packet, being careful of the steam in the packet. Remove any skin, bones, and cartilage.

7. Using a pair of forks, shred the chicken and transfer it to a bowl. Add the Pee Dee sauce as well as any needed liquid from the foil to reach your desired level of moistness.

8. Serve immediately as is, or on hamburger buns, topped with more sauce.

FRESH SMOKED HAM

SERVES 8 TO 10
PREP TIME: 15 MINUTES
BRINE TIME: 24 HOURS
COOK TIME: 4 HOURS

 SUGGESTED WOOD: **Hickory**

South Carolinians' go-to barbecue dish might be pulled pork, but in many parts of the state, they swear by fresh ham. This cut is leaner than a Boston butt, so paying careful attention to the temperatures is critical. Glazed and served with the Carolina Gold Barbecue Sauce, this will quickly become a favorite.

For the brine

2 quarts water

½ cup kosher salt

¾ cup dark brown sugar

1 tablespoon SC Barbecue Rub (page 138)

1 teaspoon whole cloves

For the ham

1 (8- to 10-pound) ham, preferably the shank portion

¼ cup SC Barbecue Rub (page 138)

2 cups Carolina Gold Barbecue Sauce (page 140), plus more for serving

1. **To make the brine:** In a container or cooler large enough to hold both the ham and the brine, combine all of the brine ingredients and stir until the salt and sugar crystals have dissolved.

2. **To make the ham:** Place the ham in the brine, cover, and refrigerate for 24 hours.

3. Preheat your smoker to 200°F with 2 chunks of wood.

4. Rinse the ham under cold water and pat it dry with paper towels. Using a sharp knife, score the skin in a diamond pattern at 1-inch intervals.

5. Place the flat side of the ham on a disposable aluminum roasting pan. Season the outside of the ham with the barbecue rub. Place the ham in the smoker and cook for 2 hours.

6. Increase the temperature of the smoker to 250°F. Baste the outside of the ham with the Carolina gold sauce, then cover it with foil.

7. Continue to cook for 1½ hours more, or until the internal temperature reaches 165°F.

8. Remove the ham from the smoker and allow it to rest for 30 minutes.

9. Trim and discard any excess fat from the ham. Slice and serve with Carolina gold sauce.

Pro Advice: If you want to serve this South Carolina ham chopped rather than sliced, go for it. Chop the pork into bite-size pieces and transfer them to a large bowl. Strain the remaining juices from the bottom of the pan and pour them into the bowl along with the Carolina Gold Barbecue Sauce, to taste.

GOLDEN PORK BELLY BURNT ENDS

SERVES 10
PREP TIME: 30 MINUTES
COOK TIME: 4 HOURS 30 MINUTES

 SUGGESTED WOOD: **Hickory**

This take on the ever-popular pork belly burnt ends uses the Carolina Gold Barbecue Sauce instead of the conventional red sauce. These pork morsels burst with flavor from the tangy mustard-based sauce and are sticky from the brown sugar.

1 (4- to 5-pound) pork belly, skin removed

¼ cup SC Barbecue Rub (page 138)

2 cups Carolina Gold Barbecue Sauce (page 140), divided

4 tablespoons dark brown sugar

4 tablespoons salted butter, sliced

1. Preheat your smoker to 225°F with 3 chunks of wood.

2. Cut the pork belly into 2-inch cubes and season thoroughly with the barbecue rub.

3. Space out the cubed pork on a non-coated wire rack. Place the rack into the smoker and cook for 2½ hours.

4. Remove the cubes from the smoker and transfer them into a disposable foil pan in a single layer. Pour 1 cup of barbecue sauce over the cubes, then sprinkle them with the brown sugar and toss until well coated. Place butter slices in the pan among the pork belly. Cover the pan with foil and return it to the smoker for 1½ hours more, gently tossing after 45 minutes.

5. Carefully remove the pan from the smoker, then remove the foil. Drain any liquid from the pan, add the remaining 1 cup of barbecue sauce, and toss until all of the pork belly is coated.

6. Place the pan, uncovered, back into the smoker for 30 minutes more, until the pork is sticky and thick.

Pro Advice: If your pork belly comes with the skin on, grab one of the corners of the skin and, with a sharp knife, carefully slice under it, making sure to tilt the knife slightly up toward the skin. Continue to pull the corner firmly as you slice away the layer of skin. Be careful not to trim away the top layer of fat.

PEE DEE PULLED PORK

SERVES 8
PREP TIME: 15 MINUTES
REST TIME: 24 HOURS
COOK TIME: 10 HOURS

 SUGGESTED WOOD: **Oak and Hickory**

This recipe features the vinegar- and tomato-based sauce of South Carolina's Pee Dee region. You'll wait until the end of the cook to wrap the meat in foil, which keeps it warm and allows the juices to mix with some of the sauce. Be sure to keep the water pan full to help keep the surface of the meat moist, allowing for the formation of bark and better absorption of the smoky flavor.

1 (7- to 8-pound) pork shoulder

3 tablespoons yellow mustard

¼ cup SC Barbecue Rub (page 138)

2 cups Pee Dee Tomato Barbecue Sauce (page 139), divided

1. Preheat your smoker to 225°F with 2 chunks of oak and 2 chunks of hickory wood.

2. Lightly trim the pork shoulder of any loose fat, being sure to leave the fat cap intact.

3. Thoroughly rub the pork shoulder down with the yellow mustard. Season the meat liberally with the barbecue rub.

4. Place an aluminum pan with water closest to the heat source inside the smoker. Place the pork, fat-side up, next to the pan in the smoker.

5. Cook for about 10 hours, until it reaches an internal temperature of 200°F. Be sure to replenish the water and wood chunks as needed.

6. Remove the pork from the smoker and coat it with the Pee Dee sauce. Double wrap the pork in foil and allow it to rest in a cooler for 1 hour.

7. Using heat-resistant rubber gloves, transfer the shoulder to a deep aluminum tray. Pull the meat into 1- to 2-inch strips, discarding the bone and any extra bits of fat.

8. Add any remaining liquid from the foil and sprinkle on more of the rub to taste. Serve with the remaining Pee Dee sauce.

Ingredient Tip: This recipe calls for both oak and hickory wood chunks. Both woods are common to the area and are mixed regularly. Experiment to find the right combination for you.

SMOKED DOUBLE-CUT PORK CHOPS

SERVES 8
PREP TIME: 15 MINUTES
BRINE TIME: 4 TO 6 HOURS
COOK TIME: 2 HOURS

 SUGGESTED WOOD: **Hickory**

The recipe uses double-cut pork chops, which means each thick chop has two bones in it. You can get them from your local butcher shop or online. For this recipe, the chops need to be brined for up to six hours to help retain moisture and impart flavor into this very lean piece of meat. Try this smoked version, or learn how to add some char (see tip).

For the brine

1½ cups hot water

4 cups apple juice

¾ cup bourbon

½ cup kosher salt

¼ cup dark brown sugar

1 tablespoon whole black peppercorns

1 tablespoon red pepper flakes

¼ teaspoon ground cinnamon

For the meat

3 (1½-inch-thick) bone-in double cut pork chops

¼ cup SC Barbecue Rub (page 138)

1 cup water

¼ cup apple cider vinegar

1. **To make the brine:** In a large pot, combine all of the brine ingredients and bring them to a boil, whisking, until dissolved. Allow the brine to cool for 1 hour.

2. **To make the meat:** Submerge the pork chops in the brine and refrigerate them for 4 to 6 hours.

3. Preheat your smoker to 250°F with 2 chunks of wood.

4. Remove the pork chops from the brine, rinse with cold water, and pat them dry with paper towels.

5. Season both sides of the chops with the rub.

6. Combine the water and vinegar together in a compression sprayer and prime.

7. Place the chops in the smoker and cook for 1 to 2 hours, depending on the thickness, until the internal temperature reaches 145°F. Spray the chops with the cider mixture every 20 minutes.

8. Remove the pork chops from the smoker and serve immediately.

Pro Advice: If you want grill marks or a char on the outside of these chops, pull them off the smoker at an internal temperature of 125°F and finish them on a 500°F grill, or sear them over a chimney half full of fully lit coals for about one minute per side. If using the chimney method, consider using heat-resistant rubber gloves, as the chimney will be ridiculously hot.

COUNTY FAIR SMOKED TURKEY LEGS

SERVES 8
PREP TIME: 15 MINUTES
BRINE TIME: 6 TO 8 HOURS
COOK TIME: 4 HOURS

 SUGGESTED WOOD: **Hickory**

Who doesn't love those huge turkey legs that you carry around the county fair? With this recipe, you can make this main attraction in your own backyard. The recipe scales easily if you wanted to make a huge batch of them for an event. When shopping, try to buy larger turkey legs, or you will need to reduce the smoking time.

For the brine

1 gallon water

½ cup kosher salt

½ cup light brown sugar

3 tablespoons granulated garlic

3 tablespoons granulated onion

2 tablespoons dried sage

1 tablespoon freshly ground black pepper

1 tablespoon paprika

½ teaspoon ground cinnamon

½ teaspoon ground cloves

1. **To make the brine:** In a large pot, combine all of the brine ingredients together and bring them to a boil, whisking, until dissolved. Allow the brine to cool for 1 hour.

2. **To make the turkey legs:** Submerge the turkey legs in the brine and refrigerate them for 6 to 8 hours.

3. Preheat your smoker to 250°F with 2 chunks of wood.

4. Remove the legs from the brine and pat them dry with paper towels. Sprinkle them lightly with the barbecue rub.

5. Place the legs in the smoker and cook for 3 hours.

¼ teaspoon
ground nutmeg

1 teaspoon liquid
smoke (optional)

2 tablespoons teriyaki
sauce (optional)

For the turkey legs

8 turkey legs

⅓ cup SC Barbecue Rub
(page 138)

1 cup Pee Dee Tomato
Barbecue Sauce
(page 139)

6. Brush the legs with the Pee Dee Tomato Sauce. Smoke for about 1 hour more, or until the internal temperature reaches 180°F.

7. Remove the turkey legs from the smoker and allow them to rest, loosely covered in foil, for 5 minutes before serving.

Ten

Alabama

The Story

The state of Alabama has arguably been made famous in the barbecue scene by the introduction of white sauce over 80 years ago. This mayonnaise-based sauce is superb on pork and chicken. Like in much of the South, pork reigns supreme in this state, but barbecued chicken has grown popular over the last 20 years. The region's pits burn through a lot of hickory wood, along with oak and pecan, which are all featured in this chapter.

Best-Kept Secrets

» My secret ingredient for white sauce includes Southeast Asian sambal oelek, which is a chili and garlic condiment. Though it's not traditional in the region, a few "new-school" barbecue joints include it in their white sauce, which takes it to a whole new level. A version can be found in the international aisle in just about any major grocery store and features a rooster on the label and a green lid.

» There are some who insist you use Miracle Whip for this white sauce, but I recommend using real mayonnaise. See if you can find Duke's Mayonnaise, a regional favorite that is made with a higher ratio of egg yolks for a much richer and creamier sauce.

Classic Side Dishes

For me, there are few things tastier on this planet than pickles, which you'll find in just about every 'cue joint in Alabama. Served on the side, atop your sandwich, or even battered and fried, these vinegary gems pair amazingly well with barbecue. There's just one rule: Stick with dill pickles and not the bread-and-butter variety popular on burgers; those can add too much sweetness to your dish.

The peppery cousin to collard greens is turnip greens, and the people of Alabama can't seem to get enough of them. Turnip greens are often cooked with variations of pork, such as salt pork, bacon, pork belly, ham hocks, and even hog jowl. Cooked low and slow in water, along with salt and pepper, the greens break down to a consistency of a thick spinach. The fat from the pork mixes with the greens, making for an incredible dish.

Though a dessert, so technically not a side dish, banana pudding can be found in just about every barbecue joint throughout Alabama. A few variations exist, but the sweet treat typically features chunks of banana, a thick custard pudding, and vanilla wafer cookies. The vanilla wafers can be used as a bottom crust, crumbled up and served on top, or both—all topped with whipped cream.

ALABAMA BARBECUE RUB

MAKES 3 CUPS
PREP TIME: 5 MINUTES

Both sweet and savory, this rub pairs well with pork and poultry, especially in dishes using Alabama White Sauce (page 159). I call for raw or turbinado sugar in this recipe instead of granulated white sugar, as it is less apt to burn and turn bitter like white sugar can.

1½ cups molasses brown sugar

½ cup granulated raw cane sugar or turbinado sugar

½ cup kosher salt

¼ cup sweet paprika

2 tablespoons granulated garlic

2 tablespoons granulated onion

2 tablespoons mustard powder

1 tablespoon cayenne pepper

1. In a medium bowl, combine all of the ingredients and mix thoroughly.

2. Store the rub in a cool, dark place in a sealable plastic or glass container for no more than 3 months. Spices will oxidize over time and will lose their flavor if stored for too long.

Pro Advice: Depending on where you live, molasses brown sugar can be hard to find. To make your own, add one tablespoon of molasses to one cup of dark brown sugar (or two tablespoons to one cup of light brown sugar) and mix them together in your food processor until fully incorporated.

ALABAMA WHITE SAUCE

MAKES 3 CUPS
PREP TIME: 5 MINUTES

A staple in Alabama barbecue cooking, this sauce originated at Big Bob Gibson Bar-B-Q in Decatur, Alabama, back in 1925. My recipe uses a Southeast Asian chili garlic condiment called sambal oelek, which isn't traditional but will make the best zesty white sauce you have ever tasted. For something more traditional, simply eliminate this ingredient from the recipe.

2 cups mayonnaise

½ cup apple cider vinegar

3 tablespoons sambal oelek

2 teaspoons Worcestershire sauce

1 teaspoon celery seed

1 teaspoon freshly ground black pepper

1 teaspoon kosher salt

1 teaspoon red pepper flakes

1 teaspoon cayenne pepper (optional)

1. In a sealable container, such as a mason jar, mix together all of the ingredients thoroughly until fully incorporated.

2. Store the sauce in the container in the refrigerator for up to 2 weeks.

Experiment: Depending on how spicy you like your barbecue sauce, I have included cayenne pepper as an optional ingredient. I like the heat level of the sambal and the tang of the mayonnaise to come through and be the stars, but some of my friends from Alabama have claimed it isn't hot enough without the cayenne.

EIGHT-DAY BRINED SLAB BACON

SERVES 4 TO 8
PREP TIME: 5 MINUTES
CURING AND DRYING TIME: 9 DAYS
COOK TIME: 3 HOURS

 SUGGESTED WOOD: **Hickory or Oak**

I am going to warn you right now: Once you make your own bacon, you'll never want to eat store-bought bacon again. I should also mention that there is no typo in the title—yes, this does take eight days to brine, which allows the curing salt to fully penetrate the meat. Note: Too much pink salt isn't good for you, so only use the listed amount.

½ cup molasses brown sugar

¼ cup kosher salt

1 teaspoon pink curing salt

1 (3-pound) slab pork belly

1. In a small bowl, mix together the brown sugar, kosher salt, and curing salt, and set aside.

2. Place the pork belly on a cutting board and pat it dry with paper towels.

3. Sprinkle half of the rub over the pork belly and gently massage it into the pork. Turn the belly over and repeat on the other side. Place the belly in a zip-top bag, removing as much air as possible, and store it in the refrigerator for 8 days, flipping the pork belly over once per day.

4. After 8 days, remove the pork from the refrigerator and rinse it under cold water. Pat it dry and return it to the refrigerator, uncovered, on a wire rack over a rimmed baking sheet for 24 hours.

5. Preheat your smoker to 200°F with 2 chunks of wood.

6. Place the pork belly in the smoker and cook for 3 hours, or until the internal temperature reaches 150°F.

7. Store the bacon in an airtight zip-top bag in the refrigerator for up to 1 week. Slice the bacon to your preferred thickness, and then cook it either on the pan or in the oven.

Pro Advice: The best part of making bacon yourself is the endless variations you can make to please your palate. There are too many variations to mention in the ingredient list, but some of my favorite additions are black pepper (two table-spoons should do it) and jalapeño pepper (six to eight thin slices of jalapeño pepper placed in the zip-top bag during step 3, making sure to get pepper slices on both sides of the pork belly).

PECAN SMOKED PULLED PORK

SERVES 8
PREP TIME: 5 MINUTES
COOK TIME: 10 HOURS

 SUGGESTED WOOD: **Pecan**

The pork rub, along with the molasses or sorghum binder, will make for an incredibly tasty bark, and this pork pairs perfectly with Alabama White Sauce. The addition of the cola will help the sugars penetrate deeper into the meat as it steams in the foil packet.

1 (7- to 8-pound) pork shoulder

3 tablespoons molasses or sorghum syrup

¼ cup Alabama Barbecue Rub (page 158)

½ cup cola soda made with cane sugar

2 cups Alabama White Sauce (page 159), for serving

1. Preheat your smoker to 225°F with 4 chunks of wood.

2. Lightly trim the pork shoulder of any loose fat, being sure to leave the fat cap intact.

3. Thoroughly rub the pork shoulder down with the molasses or sorghum syrup. Season the meat liberally with the barbecue rub.

4. Place an aluminum pan with water in the smoker next to the heat source.

5. Place the pork, fat-side up, in the smoker next to the water pan and cook for about 8 hours, until it reaches an internal temperature of 180°F. Replenish the water and wood chunks as needed.

6. Lay out a double-thick layer of foil and place the pork shoulder in the middle. Fold up the sides of the foil and add the cola on top of the pork. Completely seal the foil and return it to the smoker.

7. Cook the shoulder for 2 hours more, until it reaches an internal temperature of 203°F.

8. Remove the pork from the smoker and allow it to rest for 30 minutes.

9. Using heat-resistant rubber gloves, transfer the shoulder to a deep aluminum tray. Shred the meat, discarding the bone and any extra bits of fat.

10. Add some of the remaining liquid from the foil as needed and sprinkle on more of the barbecue rub to taste. Serve with the white sauce.

Experiment: Feel free to experiment with other dark sodas made with cane sugar.

LOAF PAN CHICKEN

SERVES 4
PREP TIME: 15 MINUTES
COOK TIME: 2 HOURS

 SUGGESTED WOOD: **Hickory or Apple**

This recipe is inspired by the great Big Bob Gibson, who started serving barbecue from his home and is credited with creating Alabama White Sauce (page 159). He kicked off a family barbecue tradition lasting four generations. This method is similar to the one used for Beer Can Chicken (page 79), without the can, and results in tender and moist meat every time.

½ cup unfiltered apple juice

3 tablespoons Worcestershire sauce

1 (3½-pound) whole chicken

1 tablespoon turbinado or raw sugar

2½ teaspoons sweet paprika

1½ teaspoons freshly ground black pepper

1 teaspoon granulated garlic

1½ teaspoons kosher salt

½ teaspoon ground celery seed

¼ teaspoon ground cumin

¼ teaspoon ground coriander

1. Build a fire using your choice of wood.

2. In a small bowl, stir together the apple juice and Worcestershire sauce. While holding the chicken over a 9-by-5-inch loaf pan, pour the mixture over the chicken, thoroughly coating the chicken inside and out. Allow the remaining liquid to drip into the loaf pan.

3. In another bowl, combine the sugar, paprika, pepper, granulated garlic, salt, celery seed, cumin, and coriander, and mix well. Coat the chicken, inside and out, with the dry rub, discarding any excess. Place the chicken into the loaf pan, breast-side up.

4. When the smoker reaches 275°F, place the loaf pan on the grill grate with the legs facing away from the heat source.

5. Close the smoker and cook for about 2 hours, or until the thigh reaches an internal temperature of 165°F. After letting the chicken cool in the pan for 10 minutes, slice into pieces and serve.

Pro Advice: If you are feeling a bit adventurous, use the pan drippings to make a gravy. Make a roux by melting two tablespoons of salted butter in a pan, then whisking in two tablespoons of flour until fully combined. Continue whisking over medium-low heat for a few minutes until the roux has the consistency of a paste. Add the pan drippings and whisk until any lumps are gone and it is the consistency of gravy.

SMOKED CHICKEN WITH WHITE SAUCE

SERVES 8
PREP TIME: 15 MINUTES
COOK TIME: 3 HOURS

 SUGGESTED WOOD: **Hickory**

Smoked chicken with white sauce is one of the most iconic dishes in Alabama. The chicken is rubbed down with Alabama Barbecue Rub, and then basted twice with Alabama White Sauce—once during the cooking process, and once when pulled from the smoker. The sweetness of the rub paired with the twang of the mayonnaise and chili garlic sauce makes what will quickly become a household favorite.

2 (3- to 4-pound) whole roaster chickens

¼ cup Alabama Barbecue Rub (page 158)

3 cups Alabama White Sauce (page 159), divided

1. Spatchcock the chicken (page 18). Pat it down completely with paper towels.

2. Preheat your smoker to 275°F with 2 chunks of wood.

3. Lightly sprinkle the barbecue rub on both sides of the chicken and place it, skin-side down, in the smoker. Cook for 1½ hours.

4. Flip the chicken over, add another chunk of wood, and cook for 1 hour more. Baste the chicken with the white sauce and continue to cook until the internal temperature at the thickest part of the breast and thigh reads 165°F.

5. Baste the chicken again with the white sauce, then remove it from the smoker and place it on a rimmed baking sheet. Loosely cover it with foil and allow it to rest for 15 minutes.

6. Cut the chicken into sections and serve with the remaining white sauce.

Pro Advice: In restaurants in Alabama that feature white sauce, the final coating is created by dunking the entire chicken in a tub of the white sauce rather than basting it as I have recommended in the recipe. To fully recreate this, double the amount of white sauce (six cups) and, using a pair of long tongs, dunk the entire chicken in a pot of the sauce prior to letting it rest.

MEASUREMENT CONVERSIONS

	US STANDARD	US STANDARD (OUNCES)	METRIC (APPROXIMATE)
VOLUME EQUIVALENTS (LIQUID)	2 TABLESPOONS	1 FL. OZ.	30 ML
	¼ CUP	2 FL. OZ.	60 ML
	½ CUP	4 FL. OZ.	120 ML
	1 CUP	8 FL. OZ.	240 ML
	1½ CUPS	12 FL. OZ.	355 ML
	2 CUPS OR 1 PINT	16 FL. OZ.	475 ML
	4 CUPS OR 1 QUART	32 FL. OZ.	1 L
	1 GALLON	128 FL. OZ.	4 L
VOLUME EQUIVALENTS (DRY)	⅛ TEASPOON		0.5 ML
	¼ TEASPOON		1 ML
	½ TEASPOON		2 ML
	¾ TEASPOON		4 ML
	1 TEASPOON		5 ML
	1 TABLESPOON		15 ML
	¼ CUP		59 ML
	⅓ CUP		79 ML
	½ CUP		118 ML
	⅔ CUP		156 ML
	¾ CUP		177 ML
	1 CUP		235 ML
	2 CUPS OR 1 PINT		475 ML
	3 CUPS		700 ML
	4 CUPS OR 1 QUART		1 L
	½ GALLON		2 L
	1 GALLON		4 L
WEIGHT EQUIVALENTS	½ OUNCE		15 G
	1 OUNCE		30 G
	2 OUNCES		60 G
	4 OUNCES		115 G
	8 OUNCES		225 G
	12 OUNCES		340 G
	16 OUNCES OR 1 POUND		455 G

	FAHRENHEIT (F)	CELSIUS (C) (APPROXIMATE)
OVEN TEMPERATURES	250°F	120°C
	300°F	150°C
	325°F	180°C
	375°F	190°C
	400°F	200°C
	425°F	220°C
	450°F	230°C

INDEX

ACKNOWLEDGMENTS

I want to thank all of those who have helped me along the way to get to where I am now. The members of the California Barbecue Association, especially Pete Lent, helped us get our start in the world of barbecue competitions. Thanks to all my friends in SoCal who were very willing tasters, especially Vince Pereda, who later became part of Team Revolution Barbecue. To our good friends at Proud Souls Barbecue & Provisions, who welcomed us with open arms and became the first retail location to sell our barbecue rubs: Thank you! Lastly, I want to thank my family for being so supportive, as none of this would have been possible without them.

ABOUT THE AUTHOR

Glenn Connaughton is the creator of the Revolution Barbecue brand. After years of competing on the barbecue competition circuit and running a catering business, his focus has been on growing the brand and sharing his love of barbecue via social media, public events, and now this cookbook. When he's not manning the grill, you can find him enjoying the outdoors with his wife, Vida, and his adult children in Colorado. Find him @RevolutionBBQ.